D1438545

FEED COMPOSITION

UK TABLES OF FEED COMPOSITION AND NUTRITIVE VALUE FOR RUMINANTS

Second Edition

MINISTRY OF AGRICULTURE, FISHERIES
AND FOOD
STANDING COMMITTEE ON TABLES OF
FEED COMPOSITION

CHALCOMBE PUBLICATIONS

MINISTRY OF AGRICULTURE, FISHERIES AND FOOD STANDING COMMITTEE ON TABLES OF FEED COMPOSITION

Representing:

ADAS
Rowett Research Institute
The Scottish Agricultural College
Department of Agriculture, Northern Ireland
Agricultural and Food Research Council
University of Nottingham
United Kingdom Agricultural Supply Trade Association

Published in the United Kingdom by Chalcombe Publications, Church Lane, Kingston, Canterbury, Kent CT4 6HX

First edition 1986.
Reprinted with amendments 1987.
Second edition 1992.

ISBN 0 948617 24 1

Printed in the United Kingdom by Cambrian Printers Ltd, Aberystwyth

Ministry of Agriculture, Fisheries and Food (1992) Feed Composition.
Chalcombe Publications, Nr. Canterbury, 99p.

CONTENTS

PREFACE

When *Feed Composition, UK Tables of Feed Composition and Nutritive Value for Ruminants* was first published in 1986 it marked a watershed in the collation of information on ruminant feeds in the United Kingdom (UK). It was the first publication which, with one or two exceptions, concerned itself only with recent high quality measurements *in vivo* of nutritive value. In addition, it gave not only mean values but indications of the likely variability and the number of determinations on which they were based. This allowed the informed user to judge more critically the likely value of similar feeds in practice, and it was envisaged that the book would be used primarily as a working document by practising nutritionists.

It was, however, also recognised that there was a need for a more detailed and extensive reference book. Accordingly such a book, entitled *UK Tables of Nutritive Value and Chemical Composition of Feedingstuffs*, was published in 1990 (MAFF, 1990). This publication included data relating to pigs and poultry in addition to ruminants, together with extensive analytical information.

The second edition of *Feed Composition* does not replace nor compete with the detailed reference book. It is essentially an updated practical working document which summarises the information currently available in the UK on the composition of ruminant feeds and their nutritive values.

The data presented in this revised publication are primarily from animal-based studies carried out at the ADAS and the Department of Agriculture and Fisheries for Scotland (DAFS) Feed Evaluation Units (Stratford-on-Avon and Rowett Research Institute, Aberdeen, respectively). Additional analytical data have been provided by ADAS Nutrition and Analytical Chemists, and the compilation of the tables represents the considerable efforts of staff at the ADAS Feed Evaluation Unit. Without all these contributions this publication would not have been possible and the ability of UK animal production to respond to the ever increasing need for improved efficiency would have been diminished.

Although the nutritional data presented are intended primarily for use in the UK, it is also hoped that colleagues overseas may find some of them helpful.

D I Givens
Director, ADAS Feed Evaluation Unit
Stratford-on-Avon,
December 1991

INTRODUCTION

Reliable data on the composition of animal feedstuffs are vital to the cost-effective feeding and production of farm animals, particularly to produce the quality livestock products being increasingly demanded by a more sophisticated consumer population. Whether in the process of diet planning, diet construction, and compound feed formulation or in the production planning of cereal, protein or forage crops, reference to these data is invaluable.

HISTORY

The first tables giving the comparative value of animal feeds are usually attributed to Thaer (1809), based on the use of 'hay equivalents', but they were derived mainly from personal experiences and only a few experiments. Wolff (1861), a feed scientist working at Hohenheim, first compiled extended tables on crude nutrients, nutrient requirements, digestibility and feed prices. Later, he published the first table with values for minerals (Wolff, 1871) and a table which included digestible nutrients (Wolff, 1894), obtained from the use of the standardised 'Weende' methods. Kellner used the same techniques in his work and compiled tables that included the chemical composition and the energy value of feeds (Kellner, 1905). A translation into English by Goodwin of *The Scientific Feeding of Farm Animals* (Kellner, 1909) introduced the concepts to the UK.

Wood, at Cambridge, used Kellner's tables to derive his own (Wood, 1917, 1918), which four years later appeared as *MAFF Miscellaneous Publication No 32, Rations for Livestock* (Wood, 1921). This later became *Bulletin 48*, whose history was surveyed by Eden and Buttress (1965) through 15 editions chiefly with W E Woodman as editor (Wood and Woodman, 1932; Woodman, 1948; Evans, 1960).

The first extensive compilations of animal feed composition data in the USA were made by Henry (1898) in his book *Feeds and Feeding* and later by Armsby (1903). Henry's book was taken over by his co-author, Morrison, to become one of the standard reference works used by animal nutritionists (Morrison, 1930). Schneider (1947), with his publication *Feeds of the World*, used strict criteria to select data for his tables, which were the first to list digestible nutrients by species of animal. Some 900 references involving 11,000 trials were reviewed.

PRESENT SITUATION

In both the UK and USA tables, however, a great deal of extrapolation from 'old' data *in vivo* took place over a number of years. It became questionable whether many of these data could be ascribed to UK feeds produced under modern conditions. For this reason, the DAFS and ADAS Feed Evaluation Units were set up in 1973 and 1976 respectively to produce new, high quality data on the chemical composition, digestibility *in vivo* and energy values of ruminant feeds.

The sets of tables in this publication have been compiled by the Ruminant Sub-Group of the Standing Committee of Feed Composition and are based primarily on data from the two Feed Evaluation Units, but they also include other material where appropriate. All the new nutritive values quoted have been determined *in vivo* using wether sheep fed at a near to maintenance feeding level.

The feeds in these tables have been classified essentially by the system of the International Network of Feed Information Centres (INFIC) and where possible international feed numbers and descriptions have been given.

GLOSSARY OF TERMS

ADF	Acid detergent fibre
AEE	Acid ether extract
Ca	Calcium
CP	Crude protein
DM	Dry matter
DOMD	Digestible organic matter in the dry matter
Dig NDF	Digestibility coefficient of neutral detergent fibre
Dig CP	Digestibility coefficient of crude protein
EE	Ether extract
Eff N Dg	Effective degradability of nitrogen at a rumen outflow rate of 0.05 h^{-1}. Where measurements are not available protein sources have been categorised into groups according to ARC (1980) recommendations, viz: A = 0.71 - 0.90; B = 0.51 - 0.70; C = 0.31 - 0.50; D = 0.31
FW	Fresh weight
g	Gram
GE	Gross energy
HT	High temperature
kg	Kilogram
Max	Maximum
ME	Metabolisable energy
Mg	Magnesium
Min	Minimum
MJ	Megajoule
N	Nitrogen
n	Number of samples
NaOH	Sodium hydroxide
NCD	Neutral detergent-cellulase DOMD
NDF	Neutral detergent fibre
NH_3	Ammonia
ODM	Oven dry matter
P	Phosphorus

SD	Standard deviation
TA	Total ash
TDM	Toluene dry matter
Tr	Trace amount
WSC	Water soluble carbohydrates

Further information on parameters determined, analytical methods, descriptions of Feed Classes and sources of data is given in MAFF (1990).

FEED CLASS 10

HAYS

Nutritive values[1]

	ME	DOMD	Dig NDF	Dig CP	Eff N Dg	DM	GE	CP
	MJ	g				g	MJ	g

Grass hay, all curing methods

	ME	DOMD	Dig NDF	Dig CP	Eff N Dg	DM	GE	CP
Mean	8.8	596	0.63	0.55	0.58	865	18.4	107
Min	5.9	362	0.54	0.29	0.58	791	17.0	52
Max	13.0	778	0.70	0.75	0.58	915	19.5	199
SD	1.0	57.4	0.06	0.11	–	25.0	0.45	34.6
n	90	124	18	111	1	119	128	128

Grass hay, barn cured (1-15-335 Grass hay, fan air dried)

	ME	DOMD	Dig NDF	Dig CP	Eff N Dg	DM	GE	CP
Mean	9.2	623	0.59	0.61	0.58	867	18.4	122
Min	6.1	441	0.54	0.33	0.58	816	17.0	59
Max	13.0	778	0.66	0.75	0.58	907	19.4	185
SD	1.4	58.4	0.05	0.11	–	22.9	0.51	36.1
n	22	51	6	45	1	47	50	50

Grass hay, barn cured, by ME

Grass hay, barn cured, ME <8 MJ/kg DM

	ME	DOMD	Dig NDF	Dig CP	Eff N Dg	DM	GE	CP
Mean	7.3	540	0.55	0.38	0.58	870	17.4	68
Min	6.1	441	0.54	0.33	0.58	864	17.0	59
Max	7.9	578	0.56	0.41	0.58	872	18.5	93
SD	0.83	66.0	0.01	0.04	–	4.0	0.75	17.0
n	4	4	3	4	1	4	4	4

Grass hay, barn cured, ME 8-10 MJ/kg DM

	ME	DOMD	Dig NDF	Dig CP	Eff N Dg	DM	GE	CP
Mean	9.0	589	0.63	0.59	–	864	18.6	113
Min	8.0	570	0.61	0.39	–	817	18.3	74
Max	9.6	614	0.66	0.68	–	894	18.9	185
SD	0.50	15.9	0.03	0.09	–	26.8	0.25	37.8
n	12	11	3	9	–	9	12	12

Grass hay, barn cured, ME >10 MJ/kg DM

	ME	DOMD	Dig NDF	Dig CP	Eff N Dg	DM	GE	CP
Mean	10.7	646	–	0.69	–	848	18.8	150
Min	10.1	599	–	0.66	–	816	18.3	98
Max	13.0	778	–	0.73	–	866	19.4	185
SD	1.1	66.8	–	0.03	–	21.5	0.41	36.1
n	6	6	–	4	–	4	6	6

[1]ME and DOMD per kg DM; digestibility values as coefficients; effective N degradability as a coefficient at a fractional rumen outflow rate of 0.05 per hour - where coefficients have not been determined, the degradability group (A to D; see Glossary of Terms, page 3) is indicated.

[2]DM as ODM per kg FW; other values per kg DM.

Chemical composition[2]

EE	AEE	NDF	ADF	Lignin	WSC	Starch	NCD	TA	Ca	P	Mg
g	g	g	g	g	g	g	g	g	g	g	g
17	**16**	**657**	**367**	**60**	**108**	**2**	**563**	**74**	**5.2**	**2.6**	**1.4**
5	14	437	207	38	8	0	417	44	1.9	1.1	0.7
38	19	820	554	91	247	7	721	118	25.0	7.8	4.8
5.1	1.9	61.5	46.2	12.1	53.5	1.8	78.2	13.6	2.5	0.77	0.52
125	5	123	123	81	85	47	84	115	128	128	128
18	**–**	**627**	**349**	**56**	**119**	**1**	**601**	**77**	**5.6**	**2.7**	**1.4**
9	–	437	207	38	13	0	450	56	3.3	1.7	1.0
38	–	725	421	80	244	6	721	117	11.3	4.0	2.1
5.1	–	60.2	45.2	11.2	60.6	1.6	63.0	15.3	1.7	0.63	0.34
50	–	50	48	40	35	27	37	37	50	50	50
17	**–**	**645**	**368**	**–**	**–**	**–**	**–**	**70**	**–**	**–**	**–**
17	–	626	358	–	–	–	–	69	–	–	–
17	–	700	397	–	–	–	–	70	–	–	–
0.0	–	37.0	19.5	–	–	–	–	0.50	–	–	–
4	–	4	4	–	–	–	–	4	–	–	–
16	**–**	**672**	**393**	**–**	**–**	**–**	**–**	**68**	**–**	**–**	**–**
9	–	654	344	–	–	–	–	56	–	–	–
20	–	701	421	–	–	–	–	87	–	–	–
2.9	–	14.4	18.4	–	–	–	–	10.8	–	–	–
12	–	12	12	–	–	–	–	12	–	–	–
18	**–**	**604**	**343**	**–**	**–**	**–**	**–**	**79**	**–**	**–**	**–**
9	–	437	207	–	–	–	–	57	–	–	–
24	–	674	389	–	–	–	–	90	–	–	–
5.9	–	88.2	70.7	–	–	–	–	12.7	–	–	–
6	–	6	6	–	–	–	–	6	–	–	–

Nutritive values[1]

	ME	DOMD	Dig NDF	Dig CP	Eff N Dg		DM	GE	CP
	MJ	g					g	MJ	g

Grass hay, sun cured (1-02-250 Grass hay, sun cured)

	ME	DOMD	Dig NDF	Dig CP	Eff N Dg	DM	GE	CP
Mean	8.7	577	0.65	0.51	–	864	18.4	99
Min	5.9	362	0.58	0.29	–	791	17.3	52
Max	10.4	677	0.70	0.73	–	915	19.5	199
SD	0.90	48.6	0.05	0.10	–	26.6	0.41	30.7
n	67	72	12	65	–	71	77	77

Grass hay, sun cured, by ME

Grass hay, sun cured, ME <8 MJ/kg DM

	ME	DOMD	Dig NDF	Dig CP	Eff N Dg	DM	GE	CP
Mean	7.4	519	–	0.44	–	859	18.2	84
Min	5.9	362	–	0.29	–	827	17.6	57
Max	7.9	598	–	0.59	–	880	19.5	120
SD	0.49	57.1	–	0.08	–	16.8	0.49	15.2
n	15	15	–	15	–	15	15	15

Grass hay, sun cured, ME 8-10 MJ/kg DM

	ME	DOMD	Dig NDF	Dig CP	Eff N Dg	DM	GE	CP
Mean	9.0	588	0.65	0.51	–	872	18.4	95
Min	8.0	527	0.58	0.08	–	816	17.8	52
Max	9.9	647	0.70	0.34	–	915	19.3	193
SD	0.50	29.9	0.05	0.71	–	25.9	0.34	26.5
n	49	49	11	42	–	43	49	49

Grass hay, sun cured, ME 10 >MJ/kg DM

	ME	DOMD	Dig NDF	Dig CP	Eff N Dg	DM	GE	CP
Mean	10.1	631	0.68	0.60	–	866	18.6	114
Min	10.0	613	0.68	0.50	–	840	18.3	75
Max	10.4	646	0.68	0.68	–	896	19.2	157
SD	0.20	16.8	–	0.10	–	28.2	0.50	41.2
n	3	3	1	3	–	3	3	3

Lucerne hay (1-00-078 Alfalfa hay, sun cured)

	ME	DOMD	Dig NDF	Dig CP	Eff N Dg	DM	GE	CP
Mean	8.5	583	–	0.75	B	865	18.2	18.3
Min	7.1	537	–	0.73		854	17.3	180
Max	9.7	621	–	0.77		876	18.7	186
SD	1.0	34.5	–	0.03		8.8	0.55	4.2
n	5	5	–	2		5	5	2

[1]ME and DOMD per kg DM; digestibility values as coefficients; effective N degradability as a coefficient at a fractional rumen outflow rate of 0.05 per hour - where coefficients have not been determined, the degradability group (A to D; see Glossary of Terms, page 3) is indicated.

[2]DM as ODM per kg FW; other values per kg DM.

Chemical composition[2]

EE	AEE	NDF	ADF	Lignin	WSC	Starch	NCD	TA	Ca	P	Mg
g	g	g	g	g	g	g	g	g	g	g	g
16	**16**	**678**	**379**	**63**	**98**	**2**	**529**	**73**	**5.0**	**2.5**	**1.5**
5	14	491	244	41	8	0	417	44	1.9	1.1	0.7
30	19	820	554	91	247	7	700	118	25.0	7.8	4.8
4.9	1.9	53.9	43.2	12.3	46.5	2.1	74.4	12.7	2.9	0.84	0.61
74	5	72	74	40	49	20	46	77	77	77	77
14	–	**709**	**400**	–	–	–	–	**71**	–	–	–
10	–	491	244	–	–	–	–	44	–	–	–
20	–	820	554	–	–	–	–	96	–	–	–
2.6	–	79.5	66.0	–	–	–	–	13.9	–	–	–
15	–	14	15	–	–	–	–	15	–	–	–
16	**16**	**677**	**378**	–	–	–	–	**72**	–	–	–
5	14	558	309	–	–	–	–	48	–	–	–
27	19	762	439	–	–	–	–	94	–	–	–
4.8	2.2	44.5	32.6	–	–	–	–	9.8	–	–	–
46	4	45	46	–	–	–	–	49	–	–	–
13	**16**	**650**	**342**	–	–	–	–	**70**	–	–	–
5	16	639	322	–	–	–	–	60	–	–	–
24	16	672	358	–	–	–	–	90	–	–	–
9.7	–	18.8	18.3	–	–	–	–	17.0	–	–	–
3	1	3	3	–	–	–	–	3	–	–	–
13	–	**493**	**375**	**107**	–	**5**	–	**96**	**15.6**	**3.1**	**1.7**
10	–	423	320	88	–	2	–	80	13.8	2.5	1.3
17	–	574	448	139	–	7	–	105	18.0	3.9	2.0
3.4	–	59.1	50.4	27.9	–	2.0	–	10.2	1.8	0.66	0.27
5	–	5	5	3	–	5	–	5	5	5	5

Nutritive values[1]

	ME	DOMD	Dig NDF	Dig CP	Eff N Dg		DM	GE	CP
	MJ	g					g	MJ	g

Lucerne hay, by ME

Lucerne hay, ME <8 MJ/kg DM

	ME	DOMD	Dig NDF	Dig CP	Eff N Dg		DM	GE	CP
Mean	**7.5**	**549**	–	**0.73**	–		**865**	**17.9**	**180**
Min	7.1	537	–	0.73	–		859	17.3	180
Max	7.8	561	–	0.73	–		871	18.5	180
SD	0.45	17.3	–	–	–		8.8	0.85	–
n	2	2	–	1	–		2	2	1

Lucerne hay, ME 8-10 MJ/kg DM

	ME	DOMD	Dig NDF	Dig CP	Eff N Dg		DM	GE	CP
Mean	**9.2**	**605**	–	**0.77**	–		**865**	**18.4**	**186**
Min	8.7	587	–	0.77	–		854	18.1	186
Max	9.7	621	–	0.77	–		876	18.7	186
SD	0.50	17.3	–	–	–		10.9	0.30	–
n	3	3	–	1	–		3	3	1

[1]ME and DOMD per kg DM; digestibility values as coefficients; effective N degradability as a coefficient at a fractional rumen outflow rate of 0.05 per hour - where coefficients have not been determined, the degradability group (A to D; see Glossary of Terms, page 3) is indicated.

[2]DM as ODM per kg FW; other values per kg DM.

Chemical composition[2]

EE	AEE	NDF	ADF	Lignin	WSC	Starch	NCD	TA	Ca	P	Mg
g	g	g	g	g	g	g	g	g	g	g	g
11	–	**547**	**421**	–	–	–	–	**89**	–	–	–
10	–	520	394	–	–	–	–	80	–	–	–
11	–	574	448	–	–	–	–	97	–	–	–
0.71	–	38.2	38.2	–	–	–	–	12.0	–	–	–
2	–	2	2	–	–	–	–	2	–	–	–
14	–	**458**	**344**	–	–	–	–	**100**	–	–	–
10	–	423	320	–	–	–	–	92	–	–	–
17	–	499	375	–	–	–	–	105	–	–	–
3.8	–	38.4	28.2	–	–	–	–	7.2	–	–	–
3	–	3	3	–	–	–	–	3	–	–	–

11

FEED CLASS 11

HIGH TEMPERATURE DRIED GREEN CROPS

11. HIGH TEMPERATURE DRIED GREEN CROPS

Nutritive values[1]

	ME	DOMD	Dig NDF	Dig CP	Eff N Dg	DM	GE	CP
	MJ	g				g	MJ	g

HT Dried grass, short cutting cycle, all species (1-02-211 Grass

Mean	10.7	666	0.78	0.70	B	917	18.5	199
Min	8.6	554	0.65	0.63		890	17.6	170
Max	12.0	743	0.85	0.77		979	19.4	262
SD	1.0	51.1	0.06	0.04		19.6	0.54	23.4
n	20	20	20	20		20	20	20

HT Dried grass, short cutting cycle, by species

HT Dried grass, short cutting cycle, perennial (Grass meal dehydrated,

Mean	10.9	681	0.79	0.70	–	916	18.6	201
Min	9.5	612	0.70	0.64	–	890	17.8	170
Max	12.0	743	0.85	0.77	–	979	19.4	262
SD	0.81	38.4	0.04	0.04	–	20.9	0.49	24.5
n	17	17	17	17	–	17	17	17

HT Dried grass, short cutting cycle, tall fescue (Grass meal dehydrated,

Mean	9.2	582	0.69	0.67	–	926	17.9	186
Min	8.6	554	0.65	0.63	–	920	17.6	176
Max	9.7	604.3	0.73	0.69	–	931	18.1	197
SD	0.53	25.8	0.04	0.04	–	5.4	0.28	10.6
n	3	3	3	3	–	3	3	3

HT Dried grass, short cutting cycle, by ME

HT Dried grass, short cutting cycle, ME 8-10 MJ/kg DM

Mean	9.4	606	0.72	0.68	–	926	18.0	194
Min	8.6	554	0.65	0.63	–	907	17.6	176
Max	9.9	651	0.80	0.73	–	945	18.3	225
SD	0.44	32.8	0.05	0.04	–	12.7	0.26	17.0
n	6	6	6	6	–	6	6	6

(1) ME and DOMD per kg DM; digestibility values as coefficients; effective N degradability as a coefficient at a fractional rumen outflow rate of 0.05 per hour - where coefficients have not been determined, the degradability group (A to D; see Glossary of Terms, page 3) is indicated.

(2) DM as ODM per kg FW; other values per kg DM.

14

Chemical composition[(2)]

EE	AEE	NDF	ADF	Lignin	WSC	Starch	NCD	TA	Ca	P	Mg
g	g	g	g	g	g	g	g	g	g	g	g

meal dehydrated, cutting cycle <36 days)

EE	AEE	NDF	ADF	Lignin	WSC	Starch	NCD	TA	Ca	P	Mg
37	**48**	**541**	**282**	**60**	**148**	–	**733**	**108**	**6.9**	**3.8**	**1.9**
12	41	303	239	29	95	–	627	75	5.0	3.1	1.1
52	57	640	329	92	226	–	815	173	8.5	4.9	2.9
8.5	6.0	66.1	26.8	16.1	43.4	–	58.6	22.7	1.1	0.44	0.52
16	8	20	16	16	20	–	20	20	20	20	20

cutting cycle <36 days, based on *Lolium perenne*)

EE	AEE	NDF	ADF	Lignin	WSC	Starch	NCD	TA	Ca	P	Mg
38	**49**	**538**	**279**	**59**	**155**	–	**751**	**102**	**6.7**	**3.8**	**1.8**
12	41	303	239	29	102	–	679	75	5.0	3.1	1.1
52	57	640	319	82	226	–	815	130	8.5	4.9	2.9
9.3	5.6	71.5	26.1	15.1	42.6	–	43.0	15.6	1.1	0.45	0.50
13	7	17	13	13	17	–	17	17	17	17	17

cutting cycle <36 days, based on *Festuca arundinacea*)

EE	AEE	NDF	ADF	Lignin	WSC	Starch	NCD	TA	Ca	P	Mg
36	**41**	**560**	**297**	**66**	**105**	–	**633**	**144**	**7.6**	**3.7**	**2.4**
32	41	552	269	53	95	–	627	123	7.2	3.3	2.4
40	41	567	329	92	125	–	637	173	7.9	4.1	2.5
4.0	–	7.6	30.3	22.5	16.7	–	5.3	25.8	0.38	0.40	0.06
3	1	3	3	3	3	–	3	3	3	3	3

EE	AEE	NDF	ADF	Lignin	WSC	Starch	NCD	TA	Ca	P	Mg
39	**42**	**574**	**296**	–	–	–	–	**130**	–	–	–
32	41	552	269	–	–	–	–	109	–	–	–
48	43	640	329	–	–	–	–	173	–	–	–
5.9	1.4	33.2	23.7	–	–	–	–	23.0	–	–	–
5	2	6	6	–	–	–	–	6	–	–	–

Nutritive values[1]

	ME	DOMD	Dig NDF	Dig CP	Eff N Dg	DM	GE	CP
	MJ	g				g	MJ	g

HT Dried grass, short cutting cycle, ME >10 MJ/kg DM

Mean	11.2	692	0.80	0.70	–	914	18.7	201
Min	10.3	638	0.70	0.64	–	890	17.8	170
Max	12.0	743	0.85	0.77	–	979	19.4	262
SD	0.56	31.4	0.04	0.04	–	21.3	0.48	26.0
n	14	14	14	14	–	14	14	14

HT Dried grass, unknown cutting cycle, all species (1-02-211

Mean	10.4	653	0.82	0.66	0.76	894	18.6	188
Min	8.0	518	0.73	0.48	0.76	841	15.0	82
Max	13.4	770	0.88	0.93	0.76	962	19.7	269
SD	1.2	57.0	0.06	0.08	–	27.3	0.59	38.5
n	110	102	14	70	1	80	114	114

HT Dried grass, unknown cutting cycle, by ME

HT Dried grass, unknown cutting cycle, ME 8-10 MJ/kg DM

Mean	9.2	605	0.74	0.62	–	899	18.3	188
Min	8.0	518	0.73	0.48	–	855	15.0	82
Max	10.0	688	0.75	0.73	–	962	18.9	269
SD	0.58	33.4	0.01	0.06	–	28.8	0.68	44.9
n	44	42	4	39	–	41	44	44

HT Dried grass, unknown cutting cycle, ME >10 MJ/kg DM

Mean	11.2	689	0.85	0.71	–	890	18.9	189
Min	10.0	611	0.81	0.61	–	841	18.2	123
Max	13.4	770	0.88	0.93	–	942	19.7	260
SD	0.78	42.7	0.02	0.06	–	25.3	0.35	33.4
n	66	58	10	29	–	37	66	66

HT Dried lucerne, all varieties (1-07-848 Alfalfa, dehydrated

Mean	8.8	544	0.56	0.67	B	895	18.7	199
Min	5.8	452	0.54	0.35		825	18.1	156
Max	12.1	643	0.57	0.75		925	20.5	268
SD	1.3	43.5	0.02	0.07		24.6	0.39	27.7
n	39	50	2	37		22	50	43

[1]ME and DOMD per kg DM; digestibility values as coefficients; effective N degradability as a coefficient at a fractional rumen outflow rate of 0.05 per hour - where coefficients have not been determined, the degradability group (A to D; see Glossary of Terms, page 3) is indicated.

[2]DM as ODM per kg FW; other values per kg DM.

Chemical composition[2]

EE	AEE	NDF	ADF	Lignin	WSC	Starch	NCD	TA	Ca	P	Mg
g	g	g	g	g	g	g	g	g	g	g	g
37	**50**	**527**	**274**	–	–	–	–	**99**	–	–	–
12	41	303	239	–	–	–	–	75	–	–	–
52	57	610	313	–	–	–	–	130	–	–	–
9.6	5.4	72.5	26.1	–	–	–	–	15.7	–	–	–
11	6	14	10	–	–	–	–	14	–	–	–

Grass meal dehydrated)

EE	AEE	NDF	ADF	Lignin	WSC	Starch	NCD	TA	Ca	P	Mg
37	**45**	**538**	**297**	**49**	**123**	**12**	**763**	**94**	**7.4**	**3.3**	**1.8**
12	20	403	177	18	39	0	616	53	3.8	2.0	1.0
52	56	692	406	149	227	106	850	280	49.8	11.8	4.6
7.9	10.9	49.1	41.3	29.8	35.7	27.0	63.1	28.1	4.9	1.1	0.47
113	9	105	105	62	63	31	47	111	114	113	112

EE	AEE	NDF	ADF	Lignin	WSC	Starch	NCD	TA	Ca	P	Mg
36	**20**	**553**	**309**	–	–	–	–	**106**	–	–	–
12	20	403	177	–	–	–	–	60	–	–	–
52	20	692	406	–	–	–	–	280	–	–	–
8.6	–	60.1	49.8	–	–	–	–	33.9	–	–	–
43	1	38	38	–	–	–	–	41	–	–	–

EE	AEE	NDF	ADF	Lignin	WSC	Starch	NCD	TA	Ca	P	Mg
38	**48**	**528**	**290**	–	–	–	–	**85**	–	–	–
18	40	459	206	–	–	–	–	53	–	–	–
52	56	631	368	–	–	–	–	133	–	–	–
7.4	6.2	39.4	33.9	–	–	–	–	19.1	–	–	–
66	8	65	65	–	–	–	–	66	–	–	–

pelleted)

EE	AEE	NDF	ADF	Lignin	WSC	Starch	NCD	TA	Ca	P	Mg
28	–	**465**	**336**	**92**	**67**	**14**	**619**	**102**	**15.0**	**3.0**	**2.3**
10	–	332	46	50	29	0	540	83	10.0	1.8	1.3
46	–	548	230	146	188	45	772	114	20.7	6.6	4.2
7.3	–	46.1	430	23.5	29.2	13.1	48.8	9.6	2.6	0.80	0.65
50	–	50	50	49	41	14	43	24	50	50	50

Nutritive values[1]

	ME	DOMD	Dig NDF	Dig CP	Eff N Dg		DM	GE	CP
	MJ	g					g	MJ	g

HT Dried lucerne, by variety

HT Dried lucerne, Enver

	ME	DOMD	Dig NDF	Dig CP	Eff N Dg		DM	GE	CP
Mean	**9.1**	**565**	**0.56**	**0.54**	**–**		**903**	**18.6**	**198**
Min	8.8	546	0.54	0.35	–		902	18.6	196
Max	9.3	584	0.57	0.73	–		904	18.6	199
SD	0.38	26.4	0.02	0.27	–		1.2	0.02	1.6
n	2	2	2	2	–		2	2	2

HT Dried lucerne, Europe

	ME	DOMD	Dig NDF	Dig CP	Eff N Dg		DM	GE	CP
Mean	**8.4**	**536**	**–**	**0.69**	**–**		**896**	**18.6**	**190**
Min	8.1	461	–	0.66	–		896	18.3	156
Max	9.0	594	–	0.73	–		896	19.0	251
SD	0.34	35.6	–	0.03	–		–	0.23	29.5
n	6	10	–	9	–		1	9	9

HT Dried lucerne, Virtus

	ME	DOMD	Dig NDF	Dig CP	Eff N Dg		DM	GE	CP
Mean	**8.7**	**541**	**–**	**0.69**	**–**		**919**	**18.7**	**199**
Min	7.9	464	–	0.63	–		911	18.2	164
Max	9.2	604	–	0.74	–		925	19.2	232
SD	0.43	37.6	–	0.03	–		5.0	0.31	21.5
n	12	21	–	13	–		6	16	13

HT Dried lucerne, by ME

HT Dried lucerne, ME <8 MJ/kg DM

	ME	DOMD	Dig NDF	Dig CP	Eff N Dg		DM	GE	CP
Mean	**7.0**	**499**	**–**	**0.63**	**–**		**863**	**18.5**	**177**
Min	5.8	452	–	0.61	–		825	18.3	158
Max	7.9	537	–	0.66	–		902	18.7	193
SD	0.91	28.9	–	0.02	–		54.3	0.16	16.6
n	6	6	–	5	–		2	6	5

[1]ME and DOMD per kg DM; digestibility values as coefficients; effective N degradability as a coefficient at a fractional rumen outflow rate of 0.05 per hour - where coefficients have not been determined, the degradability group (A to D; see Glossary of Terms, page 3) is indicated.

[2]DM as ODM per kg FW; other values per kg DM.

Chemical composition[2]

EE	AEE	NDF	ADF	Lignin	WSC	Starch	NCD	TA	Ca	P	Mg
g	g	g	g	g	g	g	g	g	g	g	g
26	–	**509**	**327**	**71**	**84**	–	**614**	**109**	**15.2**	**3.3**	**2.6**
22	–	489	309	50	73	–	597	106	14.5	3.1	2.6
30	–	528	344	91	95	–	630	111	15.8	3.4	2.6
5.7	–	27.6	24.7	29.0	15.8	–	23.3	3.5	0.92	0.21	0.0
2	–	2	2	2	2	–	2	2	2	2	2
28	–	**474**	**341**	**93**	**61**	**45**	**621**	**108**	**13.3**	**2.6**	**2.3**
23	–	411	292	81	33	45	579	108	10.3	1.8	1.6
36	–	526	401	105	92	45	662	108	17.7	3.3	3.1
4.5	–	34.1	29.2	8.4	20.0	–	30.4	–	2.2	0.55	0.44
9	–	9	9	9	9	1	9	1	9	9	9
28	–	**475**	**346**	**96**	**58**	**17**	**607**	**102**	**14.4**	**3.0**	**2.2**
19	–	426	288	66	29	4	559	86	12.3	2.2	1.7
40	–	510	416	117	92	29	682	114	18.0	4.8	2.9
5.6	–	27.2	32.4	14.9	17.7	8.7	30.3	11.5	2.0	0.59	0.37
16	–	16	16	16	13	6	16	7	16	16	16
29	–	**495**	**385**	–	–	–	–	**109**	–	–	–
15	–	449	344	–	–	–	–	104	–	–	–
46	–	548	430	–	–	–	–	113	–	–	–
12.9	–	34.4	30.8	–	–	–	–	6.4	–	–	–
6	–	6	6	–	–	–	–	2	–	–	–

Nutritive values[1]

	ME	DOMD	Dig NDF	Dig CP	Eff N Dg		DM	GE	CP
	MJ	g					g	MJ	g

HT Dried lucerne, ME 8-10 MJ/kg DM

	ME	DOMD	Dig NDF	Dig CP	Eff N Dg		DM	GE	CP
Mean	**8.8**	**554**	**0.56**	**0.68**	–		**902**	**18.7**	**198**
Min	8.0	506	0.54	0.35	–		866	17.7	161
Max	9.8	638	0.57	0.75	–		925	20.5	251
SD	0.49	28.0	0.02	0.08	–		18.4	0.45	22.9
n	29	27	2	21	–		17	29	23

HT Dried lucerne, ME >10 MJ/kg DM

	ME	DOMD	Dig NDF	Dig CP	Eff N Dg		DM	GE	CP
Mean	**11.4**	**627**	–	**0.66**	–		**874**	**18.9**	**241**
Min	10.4	627	–	0.66	–		864	18.1	214
Max	12.1	627	–	0.66	–		890	19.3	268
SD	0.69	–	–	–	–		11.9	0.46	25.1
n	5	1	–	1	–		4	5	5

HT Dried red clover (1-22-726 Clover, red, dehydrated)

	ME	DOMD	Dig NDF	Dig CP	Eff N Dg		DM	GE	CP
Mean	**8.9**	**577**	–	**0.55**	**B**		**879**	**18.7**	**177**
Min	8.9	577	–	0.55			879	18.7	177
Max	8.9	577	–	0.55			879	18.7	177
SD	–	–	–	–			–	–	–
n	1	1	–	1			1	1	1

[1]ME and DOMD per kg DM; digestibility values as coefficients; effective N degradability as a coefficient at a fractional rumen outflow rate of 0.05 per hour - where coefficients have not been determined, the degradability group (A to D; see Glossary of Terms, page 3) is indicated.

[2]DM as ODM per kg FW; other values per kg DM.

Chemical composition[2]

EE	AEE	NDF	ADF	Lignin	WSC	Starch	NCD	TA	Ca	P	Mg
g	g	g	g	g	g	g	g	g	g	g	g
26	**20**	**473**	**340**	–	–	–	–	**104**	–	–	–
16	20	382	258	–	–	–	–	83	–	–	–
34	20	528	392	–	–	–	–	114	–	–	–
3.7	–	32.6	32.0	–	–	–	–	9.5	–	–	–
29	1	29	29	–	–	–	–	18	–	–	–
25	–	**380**	**263**	–	–	–	–	**92**	–	–	–
10	–	332	250	–	–	–	–	91	–	–	–
39	–	452	277	–	–	–	–	95	–	–	–
12.2	–	45.4	10.6	–	–	–	–	2.0	–	–	–
5	–	5	5	–	–	–	–	4	–	–	–
23	–	**483**	**330**	**93**	–	**28**	–	**91**	**15.0**	**2.7**	**2.1**
23	–	483	330	93	–	28	–	91	15.0	2.7	2.1
23	–	483	330	93	–	28	–	91	15.0	2.7	2.1
–	–	–	–	–	–	–	–	–	–	–	–
1	–	1	1	1	–	1	–	1	1	1	1

FEED CLASS 12

STRAWS

12. STRAWS

Nutritive values[1]

	ME	DOMD	Dig NDF	Dig CP	Eff N Dg	DM	GE	CP
	MJ	g				g	MJ	g

Untreated cereal straws

Untreated barley straw, all seasons (1-00-498 Barley straw)

	ME	DOMD	Dig NDF	Dig CP	Eff N Dg	DM	GE	CP
Mean	**6.4**	**450**	**0.44**	**0.19**	**D**	**867**	**18.4**	**42**
Min	3.4	338	0.44	-0.07		780	16.9	20
Max	9.2	561	0.44	0.80		912	19.7	71
SD	1.2	50.0	–	0.18		26.0	0.59	12.6
n	51	53	1	28		53	53	51

Untreated spring barley straw

	ME	DOMD	Dig NDF	Dig CP	Eff N Dg	DM	GE	CP
Mean	**6.6**	**462**	**–**	**0.25**	**–**	**862**	**18.5**	**43**
Min	3.4	338	–	-0.07	–	780	16.9	20
Max	9.2	561	–	0.80	–	903	19.7	71
SD	1.4	47.5	–	0.20	–	23.8	0.61	12.9
n	30	32	–	16	–	32	32	31

Untreated winter barley straw

	ME	DOMD	Dig NDF	Dig CP	Eff N Dg	DM	GE	CP
Mean	**6.2**	**437**	**0.44**	**0.15**	**–**	**874**	**18.3**	**38**
Min	4.8	338	0.44	0.01	–	804	17.4	26
Max	8.1	527	0.44	0.33	–	912	19.4	59
SD	0.95	50.8	–	0.11	–	31.1	0.58	11.4
n	17	17	1	8	–	17	17	16

Untreated oats straw, all seasons (1-03-283 Oats straw)

	ME	DOMD	Dig NDF	Dig CP	Eff N Dg	DM	GE	CP
Mean	**7.2**	**496**	**–**	**0.07**	**0.37**	**846**	**18.2**	**34**
Min	4.9	383	–	0.00	0.37	788	17.8	20
Max	9.0	610	–	0.15	0.37	870	18.5	48
SD	1.4	73.5	–	0.08	–	31.1	0.25	10.6
n	6	6	–	3	1	6	6	6

Untreated spring oats straw

	ME	DOMD	Dig NDF	Dig CP	Eff N Dg	DM	GE	CP
Mean	**7.6**	**511**	**–**	**0.07**	**–**	**812**	**18.3**	**29**
Min	7.2	510	–	0.07	–	788	18.1	24
Max	7.9	511	–	0.07	–	837	18.4	34
SD	0.55	0.63	–	–	–	34.9	0.21	7.1
n	2	2	–	1	–	2	2	2

[1]ME and DOMD per kg DM; digestibility values as coefficients; effective N degradability as a coefficient at a fractional rumen outflow rate of 0.05 per hour - where coefficients have not been determined, the degradability group (A to D; see Glossary of Terms, page 3) is indicated.

[2]DM as ODM per kg FW; other values per kg DM.

24

Chemical composition[2]

EE	AEE	NDF	ADF	Lignin	WSC	Starch	NCD	TA	Ca	P	Mg
g	g	g	g	g	g	g	g	g	g	g	g
14	**–**	**811**	**509**	**91**	**21**	**11**	**380**	**57**	**4.2**	**1.1**	**0.7**
5	–	614	393	65	10	0	288	27	2.3	0.1	0.3
48	–	878	595	119	60	47	487	97	10.0	8.2	1.9
5.9	–	52.0	47.0	16.5	13.3	13.6	50.4	16.8	1.4	1.1	0.31
53	–	51	51	13	18	16	38	53	53	53	53
15	**–**	**811**	**505**	**91**	**14**	**18**	**389**	**56**	**4.4**	**1.3**	**0.7**
9	–	614	393	65	10	0	314	27	3.0	0.3	0.3
48	–	874	558	119	26	47	483	97	8.1	8.2	1.9
6.8	–	50.0	47.3	17.7	5.0	14.7	49.5	16.8	1.2	1.4	0.31
32	–	30	30	11	10	9	22	32	32	32	32
12	**–**	**809**	**515**	**95**	**31**	**2.2**	**362**	**57**	**3.8**	**0.8**	**0.7**
5	–	620	425	87	15	0	288	28	2.3	0.1	0.4
19	–	878	595	102	60	8	419	84	10.0	1.4	1.4
3.4	–	61.0	52.4	10.6	16.3	3.2	45.5	17.4	1.8	0.35	0.31
17	–	17	17	2	7	5	12	17	17	17	17
14	**–**	**749**	**523**	**92**	**19**	**1**	**429**	**66**	**3.9**	**0.9**	**0.9**
8	–	587	500	90	19	1	367	63	2.5	0.7	0.4
21	–	804	538	93	19	1	607	74	5.4	1.2	1.3
4.9	–	92.9	15.1	2.1	–	0.2	94.8	4.4	1.2	0.24	0.31
6	–	5	5	2	1	2	6	6	6	6	6
15	**–**	**804**	**517**	**90**	**–**	**1**	**419**	**69**	**4.5**	**0.9**	**1.1**
8	–	804	517	90	–	1	372	63	3.9	0.7	0.9
21	–	804	517	90	–	1	466	74	5.1	1.1	1.3
9.2	–	–	–	–	–	–	66.5	7.8	0.85	0.28	0.28
2	–	1	1	1	–	1	2	2	2	2	2

Nutritive values[1]

	ME	DOMD	Dig NDF	Dig CP	Eff N Dg		DM	GE	CP
	MJ	g					g	MJ	g

Untreated winter oats straw

	ME	DOMD	Dig NDF	Dig CP	Eff N Dg	DM	GE	CP
Mean	7.0	489	–	0.08	0.37	863	18.1	37
Min	4.9	383	–	0.00	0.37	853	17.8	20
Max	9.0	610	–	0.15	0.37	870	18.5	48
SD	1.7	93.8	–	0.11	–	8.0	0.28	11.9
n	4	4	–	2	1	4	4	4

Untreated winter triticale straw (Triticale straw)

	ME	DOMD	Dig NDF	Dig CP	Eff N Dg	DM	GE	CP
Mean	5.6	445	–	0.03	D	873	17.8	41
Min	5.6	445	–	0.03		873	17.8	41
Max	5.6	445	–	0.03		873	17.8	41
SD	–	–	–	–		–	–	–
n	1	1	–	1		1	1	1

Untreated wheat straw, all seasons (1-05-175 Wheat straw)

	ME	DOMD	Dig NDF	Dig CP	Eff N Dg	DM	GE	CP
Mean	6.1	429	0.56	0.23	D	872	18.2	39
Min	3.2	302	0.50	0.02		701	17.3	22
Max	9.4	541	0.70	0.70		930	19.4	78
SD	1.2	47.6	0.08	0.16		30.6	0.49	10.2
n	69	70	5	27		69	70	68

Untreated spring wheat straw

	ME	DOMD	Dig NDF	Dig CP	Eff N Dg	DM	GE	CP
Mean	5.7	426	–	0.20	–	883	17.8	37
Min	4.9	365	–	0.14	–	866	17.5	25
Max	6.3	492	–	0.25	–	894	18.3	43
SD	0.61	61.1	–	0.08	–	13.3	0.32	7.9
n	4	4	–	2	–	4	4	4

Untreated winter wheat straw

	ME	DOMD	Dig NDF	Dig CP	Eff N Dg	DM	GE	CP
Mean	6.0	429	0.56	0.24	–	872	18.2	39
Min	3.2	302	0.50	0.02	–	701	17.3	22
Max	9.2	541	0.70	0.70	–	930	19.1	78
SD	1.1	47.9	0.08	0.16	–	32.3	0.48	10.5
n	61	62	5	23	–	61	62	60

[1]ME and DOMD per kg DM; digestibility values as coefficients; effective N degradability as a coefficient at a fractional rumen outflow rate of 0.05 per hour - where coefficients have not been determined, the degradability group (A to D; see Glossary of Terms, page 3) is indicated.

[2]DM as ODM per kg FW; other values per kg DM.

Chemical composition[2]

EE	AEE	NDF	ADF	Lignin	WSC	Starch	NCD	TA	Ca	P	Mg
g	g	g	g	g	g	g	g	g	g	g	g
14	**–**	**736**	**525**	**93**	**19**	**1**	**434**	**65**	**3.6**	**0.9**	**0.8**
9	–	587	500	93	19	1	367	63	2.5	0.7	0.4
17	–	804	538	93	19	1	607	69	5.4	1.2	1.1
3.3	–	101.3	17.0	–	–	–	115.8	2.7	1.3	0.26	0.31
4	–	4	4	1	1	1	4	4	4	4	4
15	**–**	**622**	**–**	**–**	**12**	**–**	**–**	**37**	**6.2**	**2.3**	**2.3**
15	–	622	–	–	12	–	–	37	6.2	2.3	2.3
15	–	622	–	–	12	–	–	37	6.2	2.3	2.3
–	–	–	–	–	–	–	–	–	–	–	–
1	–	1	–	–	1	–	–	1	1	1	1
12	**9**	**809**	**502**	**102**	**13**	**12**	**358**	**69**	**3.9**	**0.8**	**0.9**
2	8	674	400	85	5	0	277	25	2.2	0.3	0.3
21	11	925	565	119	29	52	445	120	6.7	2.1	8.8
4.1	1.4	39.3	36.8	8.2	6.5	15.2	42	20.5	1.1	0.35	0.99
70	4	66	63	25	31	30	45	69	70	70	70
14	**–**	**818**	**535**	**–**	**–**	**–**	**350**	**64**	**4.9**	**0.6**	**0.8**
11	–	792	503	–	–	–	332	53	3.8	0.3	0.5
16	–	844	565	–	–	–	363	75	5.9	1.0	1.1
2.2	–	24.3	26.9	–	–	–	13.2	9.3	0.91	0.36	0.25
4	–	4	4	–	–	–	4	4	4	4	4
12	**9**	**806**	**499**	**102**	**13**	**12**	**362**	**71**	**3.8**	**0.8**	**0.9**
2	8	674	400	85	5	0	277	29	2.2	0.3	0.3
21	11	870	558	119	29	52	445	120	6.7	2.1	8.8
4.1	1.4	37.9	36.5	8.4	6.5	15.2	43.5	20.3	1.0	0.35	1.0
62	4	58	56	23	31	30	39	61	62	62	62

12. STRAWS (cont.)

Nutritive values[1]

	ME	DOMD	Dig NDF	Dig CP	Eff N Dg		DM	GE	CP
	MJ	g					g	MJ	g

Other straws

Untreated oilseed rape straw (1-03-863 Rape straw)

	ME	DOMD	Dig NDF	Dig CP	Eff N Dg		DM	GE	CP
Mean	5.5	416	–	0.64	D		865	18.5	62
Min	3.8	410	–	0.50			855	17.8	58
Max	7.2	421	–	0.77			874	19.2	66
SD	2.4	7.8	–	0.19			14.0	0.99	5.7
n	2	2	–	2			2	2	2

Ammonia-treated cereal straws

NH3-treated barley straw, all seasons (1-12-457 Barley straw,

	ME	DOMD	Dig NDF	Dig CP	Eff N Dg		DM	GE	CP
Mean	7.7	537	–	0.18	D		871	18.7	70
Min	6.4	446	–	0.06			843	18.0	46
Max	9.3	629	–	0.36			908	19.7	125
SD	0.81	42.4	–	0.08			19.8	0.51	17.7
n	20	22	–	17			23	21	20

NH3-treated spring barley straw

	ME	DOMD	Dig NDF	Dig CP	Eff N Dg		DM	GE	CP
Mean	8.0	551	–	0.19	–		877	18.7	78
Min	6.7	446	–	0.06	–		844	18	54
Max	9.3	629	–	0.36	–		908	19.7	125
SD	0.87	46.1	–	0.10	–		20.5	0.50	21.3
n	10	12	–	9	–		13	11	10

NH3-treated winter barley straw

	ME	DOMD	Dig NDF	Dig CP	Eff N Dg		DM	GE	CP
Mean	7.7	531	–	0.17	–		866	18.7	63
Min	6.8	496	–	0.07	–		847	18.2	51
Max	8.6	557	–	0.24	–		891	19.4	73
SD	0.62	21.0	–	0.07	–		18.1	0.37	7.4
n	7	7	–	6	–		7	7	7

[1]ME and DOMD per kg DM; digestibility values as coefficients; effective N degradability as a coefficient at a fractional rumen outflow rate of 0.05 per hour - where coefficients have not been determined, the degradability group (A to D; see Glossary of Terms, page 3) is indicated.

[2] DM as ODM per kg FW; other values per kg DM.

Chemical composition[2]

EE	AEE	NDF	ADF	Lignin	WSC	Starch	NCD	TA	Ca	P	Mg
g	g	g	g	g	g	g	g	g	g	g	g
19	–	**803**	**582**	–	–	–	–	**88**	**19.8**	**1.2**	**1.1**
17	–	727	548	–	–	–	–	71	15.6	0.6	0.90
21	–	878	615	–	–	–	–	104	24.0	1.7	1.2
2.8	–	106.8	47.4	–	–	–	–	23.3	5.9	0.78	0.21
2	–	2	2	–	–	–	–	2	2	2	2

ammoniated)

EE	AEE	NDF	ADF	Lignin	WSC	Starch	NCD	TA	Ca	P	Mg
15	–	**778**	**542**	**86**	**14**	**5**	**521**	**46**	**4.6**	**1.1**	**0.6**
7	–	598	438	62	10	0	401	28	1.9	0.4	0.3
31	–	889	601	99	20	14	622	73	9.6	7.4	1.2
5.5	–	56.8	41.9	20.8	2.8	7.5	62.2	11.4	1.8	1.5	0.24
21	–	21	21	3	13	3	14	21	21	21	21
17	–	**744**	**526**	**86**	**16**	**14**	**545**	**47**	**4.7**	**1.4**	**0.6**
11	–	598	438	62	13	14	453	34	3.2	0.4	0.3
25	–	799	560	99	20	14	622	59	9.6	7.4	1.0
4.1	–	54.2	42.6	20.8	2.8	–	57.6	8.6	1.9	2.0	0.24
11	–	11	11	3	6	1	8	11	11	11	11
16	–	**810**	**572**	–	**14**	–	**506**	**43**	**4.5**	**0.6**	**0.7**
10	–	785	538	–	12	–	456	28	1.9	0.4	0.5
31	–	829	601	–	16	–	556	73	7.7	0.9	1.2
7.0	–	17.9	22.6	–	1.7	–	41.2	15.2	2.0	0.18	0.26
7	–	7	7	–	5	–	5	7	7	7	7

Nutritive values[1]

	ME	DOMD	Dig NDF	Dig CP	Eff N Dg		DM	GE	CP
	MJ	g					g	MJ	g

NH₃-treated oats straw, all seasons (1-06-272 Oats straw,

Mean	8.0	550	–	0.26	0.39		843	18.3	75
Min	7.1	499	–	0.09	0.39		774	17.8	59
Max	8.4	587	–	0.69	0.39		875	18.5	109
SD	0.62	37.5	–	0.29	–		47.5	0.33	22.8
n	4	4	–	4	1		4	4	4

NH₃-treated spring oats straw

Mean	8.3	563	–	0.15	–		875	18.5	67
Min	8.3	563	–	0.15	–		875	18.5	67
Max	8.3	563	–	0.15	–		875	18.5	67
SD	–	–	–	–	–		–	–	–
n	1	1	–	1	–		1	1	1

NH₃-treated winter oats straw

Mean	7.9	546	–	0.30	0.39		832	18.2	78
Min	7.1	499	–	0.09	0.39		774	18	59
Max	8.4	587	–	0.69	0.39		875	19	109
SD	0.71	44.8	–	0.34	–		52.0	0.37	27.1
n	3	3	–	3	1		3	3	3

NH₃-treated wheat straw, all seasons (1-06-271 Ammonia-

Mean	7.3	510	–	0.21	0.84		869	18.6	68
Min	5.9	449	–	0.08	0.84		789	17.9	44
Max	8.5	557	–	0.39	0.84		899	19.4	90
SD	0.64	35.7	–	0.09	–		25.7	0.47	12.2
n	17	17	–	15	1		17	17	17

NH₃-treated spring wheat straw

Mean	7.4	524	–	0.25	0.84		878	18.2	75
Min	7.1	502	–	0.16	0.84		864	17.9	63
Max	7.8	557	–	0.30	0.84		885	18.6	84
SD	0.32	23.8	–	0.07	–		9.4	0.36	9.6
n	4	4	–	4	1		4	4	4

[1]ME and DOMD per kg DM; digestibility values as coefficients; effective N degradability as a coefficient at a fractional rumen outflow rate of 0.05 per hour - where coefficients have not been determined, the degradability group (A to D; see Glossary of Terms, page 3) is indicated.

[2]DM as ODM per kg FW; other values per kg DM.

Chemical composition[(2)]

EE	AEE	NDF	ADF	Lignin	WSC	Starch	NCD	TA	Ca	P	Mg
g	g	g	g	g	g	g	g	g	g	g	g

ammoniated)

EE	AEE	NDF	ADF	Lignin	WSC	Starch	NCD	TA	Ca	P	Mg
18	–	**735**	**522**	–	**16**	–	**604**	**66**	**4.6**	**1.4**	**1.1**
10	–	670	364	–	13	–	578	61	2.5	0.7	0.7
29	–	774	584	–	17	–	649	75	6.0	2.9	1.4
8.7	–	45.4	106.1	–	2.3	–	38.9	6.2	1.5	1.0	0.31
4	–	4	4	–	3	–	3	4	4	4	4
29	–	**743**	**584**	–	**17**	–	**649**	**66**	**5.3**	**0.7**	**1.2**
29	–	743	584	–	17	–	649	66	5.3	0.7	1.2
29	–	743	584	–	17	–	649	66	5.3	0.7	1.2
–	–	–	–	–	–	–	–	–	–	–	–
1	–	1	1	–	1	–	1	1	1	1	1
14	–	**733**	**501**	–	**15**	–	**582**	**66**	**4.3**	**1.6**	**1.0**
10	–	670	364	–	13	–	578	61	2.5	0.9	0.7
20	–	774	583	–	17	–	586	75	6.0	2.9	1.4
5.3	–	55.2	119.6	–	2.8	–	5.7	7.6	1.8	1.1	0.36
3	–	3	3	–	2	–	2	3	3	3	3

treated wheat straw)

EE	AEE	NDF	ADF	Lignin	WSC	Starch	NCD	TA	Ca	P	Mg
13	–	**773**	**544**	**116**	**12**	**1**	**477**	**56**	**4.9**	**0.8**	**0.8**
8	–	567	498	116	8	0	399	37	3.1	0.3	0.5
23	–	869	597	116	19	2	542	84	16.2	1.3	1.1
3.3	–	81.0	26.2	–	2.7	1.5	44.4	13.6	3.0	0.27	0.17
17	–	17	17	1	12	2	10	17	17	17	17
12	–	**782**	**549**	–	**11**	–	**471**	**64**	**4.8**	**0.7**	**0.7**
12	–	760	528	–	10	–	423	58	3.3	0.5	0.5
13	–	807	587	–	14	–	542	78	6.3	1.0	1.0
0.50	–	22.8	27.1	–	1.9	–	50.5	9.7	1.3	0.22	0.24
4	–	4	4	–	4	–	4	4	4	4	4

Nutritive values[1]

	ME	DOMD	Dig NDF	Dig CP	Eff N Dg	DM	GE	CP
	MJ	g				g	MJ	g

NH₃-treated winter wheat straw

	ME	DOMD	Dig NDF	Dig CP	Eff N Dg	DM	GE	CP
Mean	**7.5**	**508**	–	**0.18**	–	**873**	**18.6**	**67**
Min	6.2	449	–	0.08	–	837	18.0	44
Max	8.5	557	–	0.39	–	899	19.2	90
SD	0.63	41.0	–	0.10	–	18.0	0.41	13.6
n	11	11	–	9	–	11	11	11

Sodium hydroxide-treated straw

NaOH-treated barley straw, all seasons (1-00-568 Barley straw,

	ME	DOMD	Dig NDF	Dig CP	Eff N Dg	DM	GE	CP
Mean	**9.3**	**619**	**0.75**	**0.63**	**D**	**806**	**17.4**	**45**
Min	6.1	483	0.75	0.33		758	16.8	33
Max	11.3	724	0.75	0.93		875	17.8	70
SD	1.8	79	–	0.31		40.6	0.36	11.2
n	7	10	1	4		7	10	9

NaOH-treated spring barley straw

	ME	DOMD	Dig NDF	Dig CP	Eff N Dg	DM	GE	CP
Mean	**9.5**	**631**	–	**0.73**	–	**796**	**17.4**	**44**
Min	6.1	483	–	0.40	–	758	16.8	33
Max	11.3	724	–	0.93	–	845	17.8	70
SD	2.1	81.9	–	0.29	–	31.9	0.39	11.7
n	5	8	–	3	–	5	8	8

NaOH-treated winter barley straw

	ME	DOMD	Dig NDF	Dig CP	Eff N Dg	DM	GE	CP
Mean	**8.8**	**573**	**0.75**	**0.33**	–	**829**	**17.6**	**51**
Min	8.2	529	0.75	0.33	–	783	17.4	51
Max	9.4	617	0.75	0.33	–	875	17.8	51
SD	0.84	62.1	–	–	–	65.1	0.28	–
n	2	2	1	1	–	2	2	1

NaOH-treated oats straw, all seasons (1-03-285 Oats straw,

	ME	DOMD	Dig NDF	Dig CP	Eff N Dg	DM	GE	CP
Mean	**7.6**	**506**	–	–	**D**	**787**	**16.8**	**32**
Min	5.5	412	–	–		779	16.5	20
Max	11.3	664	–	–		791	17.2	38
SD	3.2	137.7	–	–		6.8	0.36	10.4
n	3	3	–	–		3	3	3

[1]ME and DOMD per kg DM; digestibility values as coefficients; effective N degradability as a coefficient at a fractional rumen outflow rate of 0.05 per hour - where coefficients have not been determined, the degradability group (A to D; see Glossary of Terms, page 3) is indicated.

[2]DM as ODM per kg FW; other values per kg DM.

Chemical composition[(2)]

EE	AEE	NDF	ADF	Lignin	WSC	Starch	NCD	TA	Ca	P	Mg
g	g	g	g	g	g	g	g	g	g	g	g
14	–	**779**	**545**	–	**11**	**1**	**481**	**53**	**5.1**	**0.8**	**0.8**
11	–	567	498	–	8	0	399	37	3.1	0.3	0.5
23	–	851	597	–	13	2	526	84	16.2	1.3	1.1
3.6	–	75.8	28.9	–	1.6	1.5	44.5	15.2	3.7	0.31	0.17
11	–	11	11	–	7	2	6	11	11	11	11

treated with sodium hydroxide, wet)

EE	AEE	NDF	ADF	Lignin	WSC	Starch	NCD	TA	Ca	P	Mg
12	–	**676**	**496**	**90**	**15**	**6**	**597**	**115**	**3.9**	**1.0**	**0.7**
5	–	627	443	70	11	1	547	92	2.3	0.4	0.3
22	–	731	535	112	20	14	651	152	5.7	1.5	1.1
4.6	–	33.0	34.5	16.4	4.5	5.2	32.1	18.1	0.93	0.37	0.30
10	–	9	9	10	4	6	10	10	10	10	10
13	–	**669**	**487**	**90**	**16**	**7**	**604**	**117**	**4.1**	**0.9**	**0.7**
8	–	627	443	70	11	1	547	92	2.9	0.4	0.3
22	–	731	529	112	20	14	651	152	5.7	1.5	1.1
4.2	–	34.4	33.8	17.3	4.6	5.1	31.3	19.9	0.84	0.41	0.27
8	–	7	7	8	3	5	8	8	8	8	8
11	–	**701**	**527**	**91**	**11**	**1.2**	**573**	**107**	**3.2**	**1.1**	**0.7**
5	–	701	519	78	11	1.2	552	103	2.3	1.1	0.4
16	–	701	535	103	11	1.2	593	111	4.1	1.1	1.1
7.8	–	0.0	11.3	17.7	–	–	29.0	5.7	1.3	0.0	0.52
2	–	2	2	2	1	1	2	2	2	2	2

treated with sodium hydroxide)

EE	AEE	NDF	ADF	Lignin	WSC	Starch	NCD	TA	Ca	P	Mg
9	–	**625**	**484**	**86**	–	**1.7**	**563**	**150**	**2.3**	**0.6**	**4.0**
8	–	569	462	80	–	0.7	528	122	0.8	0.5	1.1
10	–	688	523	89	–	2.6	601	172	3.2	0.8	9.8
1.0	–	59.8	33.6	4.9	–	1.3	36.6	25.5	1.3	0.15	5.0
3	–	3	3	3	–	2	3	3	3	3	3

Nutritive values[1]

	ME	DOMD	Dig NDF	Dig CP	Eff N Dg		DM	GE	CP
	MJ	g					g	MJ	g

NaOH-treated spring oats straw

	ME	DOMD	Dig NDF	Dig CP	Eff N Dg		DM	GE	CP
Mean	11.3	664	–	–	–		791	17.2	20
Min	11.3	664	–	–	–		791	17.2	20
Max	11.3	664	–	–	–		791	17.2	20
SD	–	–	–	–	–		–	–	–
n	1	1	–	–	–		1	1	1

NaOH-treated winter oats straw

	ME	DOMD	Dig NDF	Dig CP	Eff N Dg		DM	GE	CP
Mean	5.8	427	–	–	–		784	16.6	38
Min	5.5	412	–	–	–		779	16.5	38
Max	6.1	441	–	–	–		789	16.7	38
SD	0.42	20.7	–	–	–		7.5	0.14	0.0
n	2	2	–	–	–		2	2	2

NaOH-treated winter wheat straw (1-27-550 Wheat straw,

	ME	DOMD	Dig NDF	Dig CP	Eff N Dg		DM	GE	CP
Mean	8.6	570	0.76	0.14	D		842	17.2	36
Min	7.2	498	0.68	0.01			517	16.3	23
Max	9.6	698	0.85	0.37			923	17.9	63
SD	0.61	40.7	0.05	0.20			78.4	0.45	6.6
n	26	28	20	3			26	28	27

[1]ME and DOMD per kg DM; digestibility values as coefficients; effective N degradability as a coefficient at a fractional rumen outflow rate of 0.05 per hour - where coefficients have not been determined, the degradability group (A to D; see Glossary of Terms, page 3) is indicated.

[2]DM as ODM per kg FW; other values per kg DM.

Chemical composition[(2)]

EE	AEE	NDF	ADF	Lignin	WSC	Starch	NCD	TA	Ca	P	Mg
g	g	g	g	g	g	g	g	g	g	g	g
8	**–**	**688**	**523**	**88**	**–**	**–**	**528**	**122**	**0.8**	**0.8**	**9.8**
8	–	688	523	88	–	–	528	122	0.8	0.8	9.8
8	–	688	523	88	–	–	528	122	0.8	0.8	9.8
–	–	–	–	–	–	–	–	–	–	–	–
1	–	1	1	1	–	–	1	1	1	1	1
10	**–**	**594**	**465**	**85**	**–**	**2**	**581**	**164**	**3.0**	**0.6**	**1.1**
9	–	569	462	80	–	1	560	156	2.8	0.5	1.1
10	–	619	468	89	–	3	601	172	3.2	0.6	1.1
0.7	–	35.4	4.2	6.4	–	1.3	29.0	11.3	0.28	0.07	0.00
2	–	2	2	2	–	2	2	2	2	2	2

winter, treated with sodium hydroxide)

EE	AEE	NDF	ADF	Lignin	WSC	Starch	NCD	TA	Ca	P	Mg
9	**12**	**689**	**494**	**92**	**15**	**9**	**531**	**127**	**4.8**	**0.6**	**0.7**
6	9	629	321	44	15	2	458	93	2.5	0.4	0.5
24	16	760	536	128	15	17	612	169	6.6	1.1	1.0
3.5	1.6	41.7	40.9	16.1	–	7.7	44.9	26.4	1.1	0.20	0.12
28	20	25	24	28	1	3	27	28	28	28	28

FEED CLASS 20

FRESH HERBAGES AND FORAGES FED FRESH

08## 20.   FRESH HERBAGES AND FORAGES FED FRESH

Nutritive values[1]

	ME	DOMD	Dig NDF	Dig CP	Eff N Dg		DM	GE	CP
	MJ	g					g	MJ	g

Cabbage (2-01-046 Cabbage, fresh)

	ME	DOMD	Dig NDF	Dig CP	Eff N Dg		DM	GE	CP
Mean	13.7	781	–	0.87	B		107	17.6	207
Min	12.6	649	–	0.86			84	16.6	192
Max	14.7	843	–	0.90			119	19.1	221
SD	0.82	78.0	–	0.02			13.3	0.96	12.3
n	5	5	–	5			5	5	5

Forage sorghum/sudangrass hybrid, variety topgrass (2-04-489

	ME	DOMD	Dig NDF	Dig CP	Eff N Dg		DM	GE	CP
Mean	10.9	624	–	0.74	A		174	19.4	137
Min	10.9	624	–	0.74			174	19.4	137
Max	10.9	624	–	0.74			174	19.4	137
SD	–	–	–	–			–	–	–
n	1	1	–	1			1	1	1

Fresh grass, all species (2-02-260 Grass, fresh)

	ME	DOMD	Dig NDF	Dig CP	Eff N Dg		DM	GE	CP
Mean	11.2	710	0.81	0.70	0.71		197	18.7	156
Min	7.2	540	0.62	0.27	0.47		113	17.5	54
Max	14.1	829	0.97	0.95	0.87		424	19.9	361
SD	1.2	54.7	0.07	0.12	0.084		46.8	0.45	51.4
n	243	243	70	211	51		244	244	216

Fresh grass, by variety

Fresh grass : hybrid ryegrass, variety Augusta

	ME	DOMD	Dig NDF	Dig CP	Eff N Dg		DM	GE	CP
Mean	11.5	719	0.84	0.74	–		163	18.5	181
Min	10.6	678	0.74	0.66	–		122	17.9	127
Max	12.4	757	0.87	0.83	–		181	18.9	274
SD	0.73	27.5	0.05	0.07	–		22.1	0.38	57.9
n	6	6	6	6	–		6	6	6

Fresh grass : Italian ryegrass, variety RvP

	ME	DOMD	Dig NDF	Dig CP	Eff N Dg		DM	GE	CP
Mean	11.4	716	–	0.64	0.78		223	18.6	128
Min	9.3	624	–	0.27	0.61		141	17.9	54
Max	13.2	779	–	0.79	0.87		363	19.3	248
SD	1.0	45.3	–	0.12	0.093		55.1	0.43	44.4
n	30	30	–	24	9		30	30	24

[1]ME and DOMD per kg DM; digestibility values as coefficients; effective N degradability as a coefficient at a fractional rumen outflow rate of 0.05 per hour - where coefficients have not been determined, the degradability group (A to D; see Glossary of Terms, page 3) is indicated.

[2]DM as ODM per kg FW; other values per kg DM.

Chemical composition[2]

EE	AEE	NDF	ADF	Lignin	WSC	Starch	NCD	TA	Ca	P	Mg
g	g	g	g	g	g	g	g	g	g	g	g
17	–	**244**	**136**	**11**	**316**	**4**	**855**	**108**	**8.3**	**1.9**	**1.5**
9	–	141	119	7	284	3	833	90	4.3	1.1	1.3
28	–	586	158	17	353	6	875	134	11.8	4.5	1.8
7.7	–	191.7	14.6	4.5	30.4	1.5	22.1	18.9	3.1	1.5	0.18
5	–	5	5	4	4	4	4	5	5	5	5

Sorghum, sudangrass, fresh)

EE	AEE	NDF	ADF	Lignin	WSC	Starch	NCD	TA	Ca	P	Mg
12	–	**627**	**370**	–	–	**1**	–	**75**	**4.6**	**2.4**	**1.6**
12	–	627	370	–	–	1	–	75	4.6	2.4	1.6
12	–	627	370	–	–	1	–	75	4.6	2.4	1.6
–	–	–	–	–	–	–	–	–	–	–	–
1	–	1	1	–	–	1	–	1	1	1	1
22	–	**577**	**296**	**54**	**160**	**3**	**714**	**78**	**5.4**	**3.0**	**1.6**
11	–	415	184	8	16	0	519	18	2.3	1.7	0.5
43	–	765	483	108	285	13	865	151	5.6	5.6	3.6
5.5	–	59.2	47.7	18.9	58.3	2.6	81.0	16.9	1.7	0.68	0.56
244	–	242	242	132	186	81	182	243	242	242	242
18	–	**586**	**316**	**58**	**145**	–	**724**	**101**	**5.2**	**3.8**	**1.9**
14	–	550	280	40	84	–	639	76	3.5	3.1	1.4
22	–	637	349	80	198	–	781	127	6.9	4.6	2.3
3.3	–	37.3	26.8	16.5	42.8	–	52.7	18.2	1.2	0.61	0.33
6	–	6	6	6	6	–	6	6	6	6	6
22	–	**508**	**279**	**46**	**221**	–	**758**	**73**	**4.2**	**2.9**	**1.3**
13	–	415	184	35	171	–	646	45	2.8	1.7	0.6
43	–	592	483	65	285	–	844	104	6.0	4.4	2.4
6.2	–	56.5	66.7	9.0	46.7	–	66.9	14.7	0.69	0.66	0.51
30	–	29	29	8	7	–	17	30	29	29	29

Nutritive values[1]

	ME	DOMD	Dig NDF	Dig CP	Eff N Dg		DM	GE	CP
	MJ	g					g	MJ	g

Fresh grass: perennial ryegrass, variety Ajax

Mean	**10.8**	**698**	**–**	**0.67**	**–**		**200**	**18.5**	**125**
Min	9.4	614	–	0.56	–		144	17.9	72
Max	12.6	777	–	0.78	–		276	19.0	195
SD	1.1	56.2	–	0.08	–		41.2	0.37	39.8
n	12	12	–	10	–		12	12	12

Fresh grass: perennial ryegrass, variety Melle

Mean	**11.3**	**718**	**0.83**	**0.79**	**–**		**210**	**18.8**	**225**
Min	9.1	619	0.69	0.72	–		148	18.5	163
Max	13.5	790	0.95	0.89	–		279	19.5	361
SD	1.4	52.2	0.08	0.06	–		51.9	0.31	66.7
n	8	8	8	8	–		8	8	8

Fresh grass: perennial ryegrass, variety S23

Mean	**11.5**	**721**	**–**	**0.67**	**–**		**197**	**18.4**	**102**
Min	9.9	623	–	0.62	–		146	17.9	68
Max	13.5	799	–	0.70	–		236	18.9	138
SD	1.1	55.7	–	0.04	–		32.6	0.28	25.8
n	12	12	–	3	–		12	12	6

Fresh grass: perennial ryegrass, variety S24

Mean	**11.1**	**706**	**–**	**0.64**	**–**		**206**	**18.7**	**127**
Min	7.4	540	–	0.38	–		133	17.9	77
Max	12.5	793	–	0.79	–		424	19.3	212
SD	1.2	63.1	–	0.13	–		62.5	0.37	39.5
n	24	24	–	17	–		24	24	17

Fresh grass: tall fescue, variety Dovey

Mean	**10.0**	**659**	**–**	**0.65**	**–**		**188**	**18.4**	**143**
Min	8.8	591	–	0.49	–		155	17.8	97
Max	11.0	705	–	0.80	–		241	18.8	208
SD	0.91	42.7	–	0.11	–		33.2	0.36	42.1
n	6	6	–	6	–		6	6	6

[1]ME and DOMD per kg DM; digestibility values as coefficients; effective N degradability as a coefficient at a fractional rumen outflow rate of 0.05 per hour - where coefficients have not been determined, the degradability group (A to D; see Glossary of Terms, page 3) is indicated.

[2]DM as ODM per kg FW; other values per kg DM.

Chemical composition[2]

EE	AEE	NDF	ADF	Lignin	WSC	Starch	NCD	TA	Ca	P	Mg
g	g	g	g	g	g	g	g	g	g	g	g
23	**–**	**580**	**298**	**39**	**149**	**–**	**726**	**72**	**5.9**	**3.0**	**1.1**
17	–	498	231	23	100	–	593	56	4.1	1.9	0.5
29	–	633	354	69	224	–	840	91	7.1	5.6	1.4
3.7	–	43.9	42.4	15.3	52.7	–	102.2	11.0	0.83	1.1	0.27
12	–	12	12	11	6	–	6	12	12	12	12
21	**–**	**573**	**294**	**68**	**110**	**–**	**734**	**93**	**7.0**	**2.8**	**1.8**
18	–	533	234	57	16	–	678	81	5.2	2.4	1.5
25	–	618	325	80	193	–	800	110	8.6	3.3	2.4
2.7	–	26.6	28.7	9.4	67.3	–	38.3	9.8	1.3	0.33	0.33
8	–	8	8	8	8	–	8	8	8	8	8
27	**–**	**572**	**289**	**36**	**197**	**3**	**–**	**82**	**4.4**	**3.4**	**1.2**
19	–	510	226	8	143	2	–	66	3.3	3.0	0.70
39	–	664	373	54	244	7	–	102	6.6	3.9	1.7
6.2	–	54.8	48.4	14.6	40.6	1.9	–	10.4	1.0	0.26	0.4
12	–	12	12	8	8	6	–	12	12	12	12
20	**–**	**616**	**333**	**66**	**160**	**–**	**706**	**69**	**3.6**	**3.1**	**1.3**
13	–	502	270	28	100	–	580	47	2.6	2.4	0.8
33	–	765	389	108	224	–	840	96	4.3	4.1	1.9
5.1	–	62.3	36.0	23.7	59.2	–	83.2	13.1	0.48	0.48	0.36
24	–	24	24	12	5	–	16	24	23	23	23
20	**–**	**647**	**312**	**40**	**115**	**–**	**–**	**77**	**4.6**	**2.8**	**1.3**
17	–	605	263	36	76	–	–	62	4.3	2.4	1.1
22	–	672	345	46	138	–	–	90	5.2	3.0	1.5
2.5	–	22.5	29.0	4.0	23.4	–	–	10.4	0.33	0.21	0.17
6	–	6	6	6	6	–	–	6	6	6	6

Nutritive values[1]

	ME	DOMD	Dig NDF	Dig CP	Eff N Dg		DM	GE	CP
	MJ	g					g	MJ	g

Fresh grass: tall fescue, variety S170

Mean	10.3	672	–	0.65	A		207	18.6	152
Min	7.2	603	–	0.33			153	18.0	98
Max	11.7	723	–	0.81			267	19.1	229
SD	1.3	42.0	–	0.13			40.9	0.38	44.5
n	12	12	–	12			12	12	12

Fresh grass, by ME

Fresh grass, all species, ME <8 MJ/kg DM

Mean	7.5	564	–	0.41	A		204	18.1	97
Min	7.2	540	–	0.33			157	17.8	95
Max	7.8	603	–	0.49			265	18.2	98
SD	0.32	33.9	–	0.12			55.3	0.23	2.1
n	3	3	–	2			3	3	2

Fresh grass, all species, ME 8-10 MJ/kg DM

Mean	9.5	637	0.71	0.62	0.62		218	18.5	120
Min	8.7	580	0.62	0.32	0.47		113	17.8	71
Max	10.0	757	0.82	0.80	0.73		348	19.2	256
SD	0.34	31.2	0.06	0.09	0.095		49.6	0.36	41.1
n	38	38	8	31	8		38	38	34

Fresh grass, all species, ME 10-12 MJ/kg DM

Mean	11.1	707	0.81	0.70	0.71		192	18.7	150
Min	10.0	623	0.70	0.38	0.59		122	17.9	54
Max	12.0	780	0.93	0.95	0.86		424	19.8	274
SD	0.54	34.4	0.05	0.10	0.073		47.1	0.40	44.8
n	137	137	46	117	24		137	137	119

Fresh grass, all species, ME >12 MJ/kg DM

Mean	12.6	765	0.89	0.77	0.75		193	18.9	190
Min	12.0	648	0.80	0.27	0.61		117	17.5	72
Max	14.1	829	0.97	0.89	0.87		363	19.9	361
SD	0.49	31.2	0.05	0.09	0.063		41.9	0.53	49.9
n	65	65	16	61	18		65	65	61

[1]ME and DOMD per kg DM; digestibility values as coefficients; effective N degradability as a coefficient at a fractional rumen outflow rate of 0.05 per hour - where coefficients have not been determined, the degradability group (A to D; see Glossary of Terms, page 3) is indicated.

[2]DM as ODM per kg FW; other values per kg DM.

Chemical composition[(2)]

EE	AEE	NDF	ADF	Lignin	WSC	Starch	NCD	TA	Ca	P	Mg
g	g	g	g	g	g	g	g	g	g	g	g
20	–	**613**	**303**	**41**	**109**	–	**683**	**82**	**5.1**	**2.7**	**1.5**
17	–	543	263	34	62	–	550	70	4.5	2.1	1.3
29	–	656	335	55	161	–	763	95	6.2	4.4	1.7
3.6	–	27.8	24.8	6.6	29.9	–	67.3	8.6	0.51	0.64	0.15
12	–	12	12	7	7	–	9	12	12	12	12
16	–	**659**	**351**	–	–	–	–	**69**	–	–	–
11	–	647	316	–	–	–	–	59	–	–	–
21	–	673	379	–	–	–	–	78	–	–	–
5.0	–	13.2	32.2	–	–	–	–	9.5	–	–	–
3	–	3	3	–	–	–	–	3	–	–	–
19	–	**627**	**329**	–	–	–	–	**69**	–	–	–
11	–	519	240	–	–	–	–	18	–	–	–
33	–	687	381	–	–	–	–	105	–	–	–
4.9	–	40.8	32.2	–	–	–	–	13.3	–	–	–
38	–	37	37	–	–	–	–	38	–	–	–
21	–	**582**	**301**	–	–	–	–	**78**	–	–	–
12	–	420	195	–	–	–	–	47	–	–	–
39	–	765	483	–	–	–	–	151	–	–	–
5.1	–	53.2	44.0	–	–	–	–	17	–	–	–
137	–	136	136	–	–	–	–	136	–	–	–
25	–	**535**	**264**	–	–	–	–	**84**	–	–	–
16	–	415	184	–	–	–	–	45	–	–	–
43	–	619	398	–	–	–	–	150	–	–	–
5.3	–	51.0	44.2	–	–	–	–	16.8	–	–	–
65	–	65	65	–	–	–	–	65	–	–	–

Nutritive values[1]

	ME	DOMD	Dig NDF	Dig CP	Eff N Dg		DM	GE	CP
	MJ	g					g	MJ	g

Kale, by variety

Kale, Bittern (2-02-446 Kale, fresh, variety Bittern)

Mean	11.8	754	–	0.85	B		133	17.2	164
Min	11.2	739	–	0.83			115	17.0	151
Max	12.4	768	–	0.86			152	17.3	176
SD	0.90	20.4	–	0.02			26.1	0.24	17.6
n	2	2	–	2			2	2	2

Kale, Dwarf Thousand Head (2-23-733 Kale, Thousand Head, dwarf)

Mean	11.6	756	–	0.82	B		158	17.4	158
Min	11.6	756	–	0.82			158	17.4	158
Max	11.6	756	–	0.82			158	17.4	158
SD	–	–	–	–			–	–	–
n	1	1	–	1			1	1	1

Kale, Maris Kestrel (2-02-446 Kale, fresh, variety Maris Kestrel)

Mean	12.7	789	–	0.86	B		135	17.2	166
Min	12.6	783	–	0.83			134	16.9	143
Max	12.8	796	–	0.88			136	17.5	190
SD	0.13	8.8	–	0.04			1.6	0.43	33.4
n	2	2	–	2			2	2	2

Kale, Marrow Stem (2-02-456 Kale, marrow, fresh)

Mean	11.0	670	–	0.84	B		118	16.7	152
Min	10.7	620	–	0.82			116	16.7	146
Max	11.2	719	–	0.85			119	16.8	158
SD	0.36	69.8	–	0.02			2.3	0.09	8.2
n	2	2	–	2			2	2	2

Kale, Merlin (2-02-446 Kale, fresh, variety Merlin)

Mean	11.9	770	–	0.84	B		121	16.7	147
Min	11.9	770	–	0.84			121	16.7	147
Max	11.9	770	–	0.84			121	16.7	147
SD	–	–	–	–			–	–	–
n	1	1	–	1			1	1	1

[1]ME and DOMD per kg DM; digestibility values as coefficients; effective N degradability as a coefficient at a fractional rumen outflow rate of 0.05 per hour - where coefficients have not been determined, the degradability group (A to D; see Glossary of Terms, page 3) is indicated.

[2]DM as ODM per kg FW; other values per kg DM.

Chemical composition[(2)]

EE	AEE	NDF	ADF	Lignin	WSC	Starch	NCD	TA	Ca	P	Mg
g	g	g	g	g	g	g	g	g	g	g	g
22	**–**	**258**	**207**	**23**	**233**	**9**	**804**	**115**	**12.5**	**3.9**	**1.5**
20	–	221	186	23	178	9	804	103	12.4	3.5	1.4
24	–	294	227	23	289	9	804	126	12.6	4.2	1.5
3.0	–	51.5	28.7	–	78.3	–	–	16.3	0.14	0.50	0.07
2	–	2	2	1	2	1	1	2	2	2	2
20	**–**	**236**	**201**	**23**	**267**	**5**	**788**	**105**	**12.2**	**4.2**	**1.5**
20	–	236	201	23	267	5	788	105	12.2	4.2	1.5
20	–	236	201	23	267	5	788	105	12.2	4.2	1.5
–	–	–	–	–	–	–	–	–	–	–	–
1	–	1	1	1	1	1	1	1	1	1	1
18	**–**	**232**	**182**	**17**	**302**	**4**	**814**	**118**	**12.5**	**4.1**	**1.6**
18	–	200	173	17	302	4	814	118	12.1	3.5	1.4
19	–	264	191	17	302	4	814	118	12.8	4.6	1.8
0.6	–	45.1	12.4	–	–	–	–	0.4	0.50	0.78	0.28
2	–	2	2	1	1	1	1	2	2	2	2
19	**–**	**350**	**243**	**34**	**201**	**5**	**736**	**175**	**14.5**	**4.2**	**1.8**
17	–	268	228	34	159	5	736	124	12.8	3.9	1.8
21	–	433	258	34	244	5	736	227	16.1	4.4	1.8
2.7	–	117.0	21.2	–	59.9	–	–	73.0	2.3	0.35	0.0
2	–	2	2	1	2	1	1	2	2	2	2
18	**–**	**229**	**199**	**22**	**269**	**7**	**787**	**124**	**15.5**	**4.3**	**1.7**
18	–	229	199	22	269	7	787	124	15.5	4.3	1.7
18	–	229	199	22	269	7	787	124	15.5	4.3	1.7
–	–	–	–	–	–	–	–	–	–	–	–
1	–	1	1	1	1	1	1	1	1	1	1

20. FRESH HERBAGES AND FORAGES FED FRESH (cont.)

Nutritive values[1]

	ME	DOMD	Dig NDF	Dig CP	Eff N Dg	DM	GE	CP
	MJ	g				g	MJ	g

Kale, Thousand Head (2-23-733 Kale, Thousand Head, fresh)

Mean	**11.9**	**765**	–	**0.85**	**B**	**143**	**17.3**	**188**
Min	11.2	743	–	0.85		137	17.1	136
Max	12.6	787	–	0.85		149	17.6	239
SD	0.95	31.2	–	0.0		8.6	0.38	72.8
n	2	2	–	2		2	2	2

White clover, variety Blanca (2-01-468 Clover, white, fresh)

Mean	**11.6**	**699**	–	–	**A**	**118**	**19.6**	**298**
Min	11.4	684	–	–		112	19.4	294
Max	11.7	715	–	–		123	19.8	301
SD	0.25	21.8	–	–		7.8	0.28	5.0
n	2	2	–	–		2	2	2

[1]ME and DOMD per kg DM; digestibility values as coefficients; effective N degradability as a coefficient at a fractional rumen outflow rate of 0.05 per hour - where coefficients have not been determined, the degradability group (A to D; see Glossary of Terms, page 3) is indicated.

[2]DM as ODM per kg FW; other values per kg DM.

Chemical composition[2]

EE	AEE	NDF	ADF	Lignin	WSC	Starch	NCD	TA	Ca	P	Mg
g	g	g	g	g	g	g	g	g	g	g	g
20	**–**	**259**	**198**	**16**	**321**	**4**	**825**	**117**	**12.5**	**4.2**	**1.6**
19	–	198	169	16	321	4	825	108	12.0	3.7	1.4
22	–	321	227	16	321	4	825	126	12.9	4.7	1.7
2.5	–	87.2	41.0	–	–	–	–	12.7	0.64	0.71	0.21
2	–	2	2	1	1	1	1	2	2	2	2
26	**–**	**400**	**253**	**68**	**84**	**–**	**–**	**93**	**16.2**	**3.8**	**2.2**
22	–	378	238	64	51	–	–	83	15.3	3.6	1.8
29	–	421	267	72	116	–	–	102	17.1	4.0	2.5
5.0	–	30.4	20.5	5.7	46.0	–	–	13.4	1.3	0.28	0.50
2	–	2	2	2	2	–	–	2	2	2	2

FEED CLASS 30

SILAGES

Nutritive values[1]

	ME	DOMD	Dig NDF	Dig CP	Eff N Dg	ODM	TDM	GE	CP
	MJ	g				g	g	MJ	g

Barley whole-crop silage (3-00-512 Barley, silage)

Mean	9.1	608	–	0.40	A	394	415	17.9	90
Min	6.0	509	–	0.30		199	230	17.0	80
Max	10.9	691	–	0.56		520	528	19.2	106
SD	2.1	77.6	–	0.12		137	128.5	0.95	12.0
n	4	4	–	4		4	4	4	4

Bean whole-crop silage (3-00-590 Bean, silage)

Mean	7.3	513	–	0.67	A	229	237	17.0	173
Min	7.1	493	–	0.66		216	223	16.5	168
Max	7.5	534	–	0.67		241	251	17.5	177
SD	0.26	29.5	–	0.01		17.7	19.8	0.72	6.4
n	2	2	–	2		2	2	2	2

Clover silage, mixed (Clover, mixed species, silage)

Mean	9.8	644	–	0.74	0.76	217	236	18.0	234
Min	8.5	564	–	0.65	0.75	156	182	16.2	165
Max	11.8	735	–	0.81	0.78	301	322	21.7	395
SD	1.1	56.6	–	0.05	0.017	43.2	42.8	1.5	64.3
n	10	10	–	9	3	10	10	10	10

Grass silage (3-02-222 Grass, silage)

Mean	10.9	678	0.76	0.67	0.78	255	280	19.0	168
Min	7.0	491	0.61	0.34	0.63	159	175	14.7	82
Max	14.0	782	0.90	0.82	0.90	622	629	21.7	303
SD	1.2	56.4	0.07	0.10	0.078	80.3	80.3	0.97	39.0
n	218	218	49	184	16	231	218	218	231

Grass silage, big bale (3-02-222 Grass, silage, baled and bagged

Mean	10.3	641	0.76	0.65	0.73	350	368	18.9	159
Min	7.0	515	0.66	0.39	0.63	173	195	15.9	82
Max	14.0	774	0.90	0.80	0.86	622	629	21.0	249
SD	1.4	58.6	0.09	0.10	0.097	113.1	110.4	1.1	48.7
n	31	31	10	32	4	32	31	31	32

[1]ME and DOMD per kg TDM; digestibility values as coefficients; effective N degradability as a coefficient at a fractional outflow rate of 0.05 per hour - where coefficients have not been determined, the degradability group (A to D; see Glossary of Terms, page 3) is indicated.

[2]DM as ODM and TDM per kg FW; GE per kg TDM; other values per kg ODM.

Chemical composition[2]

EE	AEE	NDF	ADF	Lignin	WSC	Starch	NCD	TA	Ca	P	Mg
g	g	g	g	g	g	g	g	g	g	g	g
20	**–**	**575**	**274**	**106**	**33**	**234**	**–**	**78**	**2.4**	**2.3**	**0.9**
13	–	485	216	106	33	171	–	41	1.5	2.0	0.7
32	–	669	308	106	33	285	–	126	3.2	2.7	0.9
8.5	–	82.9	40.7	–	–	47.2	–	37.1	0.81	0.32	0.10
4	–	4	4	1	1	4	–	4	4	4	4
13	**–**	**566**	**500**	**–**	**31**	**2**	**–**	**123**	**6.5**	**3.4**	**1.7**
12	–	543	477	–	14	2	–	120	6.3	3.4	1.6
13	–	588	523	–	47	2	–	126	6.6	3.4	1.7
0.7	–	31.8	32.5	–	23.3	0.3	–	4.2	0.21	0.0	0.07
2	–	2	2	–	2	2	–	2	2	2	2
36	**–**	**440**	**342**	**72**	**20**	**2**	**–**	**116**	**16.7**	**3.1**	**2.3**
15	–	294	266	55	20	1	–	93	8.9	2.2	1.4
54	–	564	408	89	20	4	–	156	25.5	4.2	3.7
11.7	–	75.2	45.6	24.4	–	2.4	–	19.0	5.5	0.60	0.75
10	–	10	9	2	1	2	–	10	10	10	10
43	**43**	**582**	**363**	**54**	**21**	**10**	**642**	**93**	**6.4**	**3.2**	**1.7**
15	28	399	226	25	1	0	407	54	1.9	1.6	0.7
90	68	855	513	127	220	302	801	183	16.9	5.3	3.5
11.4	12.1	69.4	46.8	17.9	29.8	38.8	71.0	17.4	1.9	0.64	0.54
226	14	217	204	137	143	66	134	231	231	231	231

or wrapped)

EE	AEE	NDF	ADF	Lignin	WSC	Starch	NCD	TA	Ca	P	Mg
31	**40**	**605**	**358**	**67**	**43**	**4**	**595**	**91**	**6.3**	**3.1**	**1.9**
15	28	485	290	43	3	1	407	58	1.9	1.7	0.9
47	55	723	450	95	220	23	749	130	11.0	4.5	3.4
9.2	13.9	57.0	38.3	15.3	52.6	7.8	70.2	16.5	2.0	0.72	0.68
32	4	32	31	31	21	8	32	32	32	32	32

Nutritive values[1]

	ME	DOMD	Dig NDF	Dig CP	Eff N Dg	ODM	TDM	GE	CP
	MJ	g				g	g	MJ	g

Grass silage, big bale, by ME

Grass silage, big bale, ME 8-10 MJ/kg ODM

	ME	DOMD	Dig NDF	Dig CP	Eff N Dg	ODM	TDM	GE	CP
Mean	8.8	608	0.69	0.60	0.63	390	406	18.1	151
Min	8.1	544	0.69	0.39	0.63	206	227	15.9	93
Max	9.6	658	0.69	0.71	0.63	580	585	19.3	223
SD	0.57	37.4	–	0.11	–	130.0	123.3	1.1	48.4
n	8	8	1	8	1	8	8	8	8

Grass silage, big bale, ME 10-12 MJ/kg ODM

	ME	DOMD	Dig NDF	Dig CP	Eff N Dg	ODM	TDM	GE	CP
Mean	10.6	639	0.74	0.65	0.71	360	378	19.2	160
Min	9.4	557	0.66	0.48	0.69	189	212	17.7	82
Max	11.5	710	0.90	0.80	0.72	622	629	20.9	249
SD	0.59	36.9	0.09	0.09	0.021	99.5	98.0	0.70	49.8
n	17	17	5	18	2	18	17	17	18

Grass silage, big bale, ME 12-14 MJ/kg ODM

	ME	DOMD	Dig NDF	Dig CP	Eff N Dg	ODM	TDM	GE	CP
Mean	12.2	729	0.80	0.76	0.86	230	255	19.4	180
Min	11.3	675	0.71	0.73	0.86	173	195	17.7	106
Max	14.0	774	0.88	0.78	0.86	339	367	21.0	228
SD	1.1	44.0	0.08	0.02	–	64.7	67.6	1.2	45.6
n	5	5	4	5	1	5	5	5	5

Grass silage, clamp (3-02-222 Grass, silage, ensiled in bunker)

	ME	DOMD	Dig NDF	Dig CP	Eff N Dg	ODM	TDM	GE	CP
Mean	11.0	684	0.76	0.67	0.80	242	267	19.0	170
Min	7.0	491	0.61	0.34	0.70	159	175	14.7	87
Max	13.7	782	0.85	0.82	0.90	515	522	21.7	303
SD	1.2	53.2	0.06	0.10	0.062	63.1	64.3	0.97	37.5
n	180	180	31	138	11	185	180	180	185

Grass silage, clamp, by ME

Grass silage, clamp, ME 8-10 MJ/kg ODM

	ME	DOMD	Dig NDF	Dig CP	Eff N Dg	ODM	TDM	GE	CP
Mean	8.4	572	–	0.54	–	327	351	18.0	160
Min	7.0	491	–	0.34	–	168	211	14.7	106
Max	9.0	675	–	0.81	–	515	522	20.2	291
SD	0.60	57.5	–	0.15	–	106.6	100.6	1.3	55.3
n	12	12	–	12	–	12	12	12	12

[1]ME and DOMD per kg TDM; digestibility values as coefficients; effective N degradability as a coefficient at a fractional outflow rate of 0.05 per hour - where coefficients have not been determined, the degradability group (A to D; see Glossary of Terms, page 3) is indicated.

[2]DM as ODM and TDM per kg FW; GE per kg TDM; other values per kg ODM.

Chemical composition[2]

EE	AEE	NDF	ADF	Lignin	WSC	Starch	NCD	TA	Ca	P	Mg
g	g	g	g	g	g	g	g	g	g	g	g
28	–	**626**	**363**	–	–	–	–	**90**	–	–	–
15	–	559	300	–	–	–	–	71	–	–	–
39	–	667	406	–	–	–	–	114	–	–	–
8.5	–	43.4	32.1	–	–	–	–	16.0	–	–	–
8	–	8	8	–	–	–	–	8	–	–	–
32	**28**	**609**	**356**	–	–	–	–	**89**	–	–	–
16	28	511	290	–	–	–	–	58	–	–	–
47	28	685	450	–	–	–	–	130	–	–	–
9.4	0.0	48.5	41.4	–	–	–	–	17.6	–	–	–
18	2	18	17	–	–	–	–	18	–	–	–
37	**52**	**535**	**341**	–	–	–	–	**97**	–	–	–
24	48	485	312	–	–	–	–	78	–	–	–
42	55	575	357	–	–	–	–	110	–	–	–
7.4	5.0	39.2	20.2	–	–	–	–	16.0	–	–	–
5	2	5	5	–	–	–	–	5			
45	**39**	**578**	**363**	**49**	**18**	**8**	**659**	**93**	**6.4**	**3.2**	**1.7**
22	31	399	226	25	1	0	480	54	4.0	2.0	0.7
90	49	855	475	127	132	302	801	183	16.9	5.3	3.5
10.7	9.3	70.1	46.5	15.8	23.0	42.9	59.1	17.7	2.0	0.62	0.51
185	3	174	165	100	109	49	90	185	185	185	185
31	–	**603**	**387**	–	–	–	–	**98**	–	–	–
23	–	399	361	–	–	–	–	71	–	–	–
40	–	692	413	–	–	–	–	140	–	–	–
4.6	–	78.7	20.4	–	–	–	–	22.8	–	–	–
12	–	10	9	–	–	–	–	12	–	–	–

Nutritive values[1]

	ME	DOMD	Dig NDF	Dig CP	Eff N Dg	ODM	TDM	GE	CP
	MJ	g				g	g	MJ	g

Grass silage, clamp, ME 10-12 MJ/kg ODM

	ME	DOMD	Dig NDF	Dig CP	Eff N Dg	ODM	TDM	GE	CP
Mean	10.3	660	0.69	0.65	0.79	249	274	18.8	165
Min	8.8	582	0.61	0.45	0.74	163	175	16.0	87
Max	12.5	729	0.74	0.77	0.86	448	460	21.6	299
SD	0.63	34.2	0.05	0.07	0.050	61.2	64.7	0.95	38.5
n	63	63	6	55	6	66	63	63	66

Grass silage, clamp, ME 12-14 MJ/kg ODM

	ME	DOMD	Dig NDF	Dig CP	Eff N Dg	ODM	TDM	GE	CP
Mean	11.7	712	0.78	0.71	0.81	227	252	19.3	174
Min	10.4	609	0.66	0.42	0.70	159	183	17.0	103
Max	13.7	782	0.85	0.82	0.90	446	474	21.7	303
SD	0.64	35.1	0.05	0.08	0.080	48.7	49.9	0.83	34.1
n	105	105	25	71	5	107	105	105	107

Lucerne silage (3-00-212 Alfalfa, silage)

	ME	DOMD	Dig NDF	Dig CP	Eff N Dg	ODM	TDM	GE	CP
Mean	8.0	557	–	0.68	0.86	338	360	18.5	194
Min	3.6	492	–	0.56	0.84	238	267	17.1	149
Max	10.2	623	–	0.76	0.87	512	523	19.4	230
SD	2.0	45.7	–	0.06	0.015	101.3	94.2	0.82	27.4
n	8	8	–	8	3	8	8	8	8

Maize silage (3-02-822 Maize, silage)

	ME	DOMD	Dig NDF	Dig CP	Eff N Dg	ODM	TDM	GE	CP
Mean	10.5	743	0.61	0.61	0.81	352	278	18.2	101
Min	7.2	583	0.53	0.51	0.81	161	191	16.3	82
Max	12.1	842	0.69	0.71	0.81	317	350	19.1	154
SD	1.1	70.7	0.06	0.08	–	47.2	45.9	0.73	15.9
n	26	26	5	10	1	26	26	26	26

Maize silage, by ME

Maize silage, ME 8-10 MJ/kg ODM

	ME	DOMD	Dig NDF	Dig CP	Eff N Dg	ODM	TDM	GE	CP
Mean	8.8	673	–	0.56	–	251	273	17.2	101
Min	8.5	652	–	0.51	–	233	260	16.3	100
Max	9.2	693	–	0.60	–	268	286	18.1	101
SD	0.50	28.9	–	0.06	–	24.7	18.4	1.3	0.71
n	2	2	–	2	–	2	2	2	2

[1]ME and DOMD per kg TDM; digestibility values as coefficients; effective N degradability as a coefficient at a fractional outflow rate of 0.05 per hour - where coefficients have not been determined, the degradability group (A to D; see Glossary of Terms, page 3) is indicated.

[2]DM as ODM and TDM per kg FW; GE per kg TDM; other values per kg ODM.

Chemical composition[2]

EE	AEE	NDF	ADF	Lignin	WSC	Starch	NCD	TA	Ca	P	Mg
g	g	g	g	g	g	g	g	g	g	g	g
42	**49**	**596**	**365**	–	–	–	–	**94**	–	–	–
22	49	443	270	–	–	–	–	54	–	–	–
63	49	855	475	–	–	–	–	183	–	–	–
8.5	–	77.3	50.7	–	–	–	–	21.4	–	–	–
66	1	59	56	–	–	–	–	66	–	–	–
47	**34**	**566**	**359**	–	–	–	–	**91**	–	–	–
23	31	420	226	–	–	–	–	62	–	–	–
90	36	683	441	–	–	–	–	138	–	–	–
10.9	3.5	62.7	45.4	–	–	–	–	14.1	–	–	–
107	2	105	100	–	–	–	–	107	–	–	–
25	–	**495**	**406**	**75**	**12**	**4**	–	**105**	**17.6**	**3.0**	**1.8**
18	–	403	342	74	4	2	–	95	13.5	2.3	1.4
33	–	606	531	76	20	7	–	119	24.0	3.4	2.1
4.4	–	81.9	77.5	1.4	11.3	2.3	–	8.5	3.4	0.35	0.23
8	–	6	6	2	2	3	–	8	8	7	8
29	–	**480**	**277**	**33**	**5**	**206**	**554**	**54**	**4.3**	**2.6**	**2.2**
14	–	376	217	19	3	8	533	39	1.7	1.5	0.7
39	–	680	386	68	7	336	573	92	11.9	6.1	3.2
6.7	–	90.8	51.3	14.8	1.4	103.8	17.9	13.0	2.0	1.2	0.69
26	–	25	25	22	6	22	5	26	26	26	26
28	–	**481**	**253**	–	–	–	–	**50**	–	–	–
27	–	457	240	–	–	–	–	48	–	–	–
28	–	504	265	–	–	–	–	52	–	–	–
0.71	–	33.2	17.7	–	–	–	–	2.8	–	–	–
2	–	2	2	–	–	–	–	2	–	–	–

Nutritive values[1]

	ME	DOMD	Dig NDF	Dig CP	Eff N Dg	ODM	TDM	GE	CP
	MJ	g				g	g	MJ	g

Maize silage, ME 10-12 MJ/kg ODM

	ME	DOMD	Dig NDF	Dig CP	Eff N Dg	ODM	TDM	GE	CP
Mean	**10.2**	**718**	**0.63**	**0.61**	**0.81**	**241**	**268**	**18.1**	**104**
Min	9.0	633	0.59	0.51	0.81	161	191	16.5	82
Max	10.8	814	0.69	0.71	0.81	316	336	19.1	154
SD	0.63	56.6	0.06	0.09	–	47.1	43.4	0.77	20.9
n	11	11	3	6	1	11	11	11	11

Maize silage, ME 12-14 MJ/kg ODM

	ME	DOMD	Dig NDF	Dig CP	Eff N Dg	ODM	TDM	GE	CP
Mean	**11.3**	**790**	**0.65**	**0.68**	**–**	**267**	**295**	**18.6**	**98**
Min	10.4	655	0.65	0.68	–	166	195	18.3	82
Max	12.1	842	0.65	0.68	–	317	350	18.8	119
SD	0.45	46.6	–	–	–	46.9	46.1	0.16	12.3
n	12	12	1	1	–	12	12	12	12

Pea whole-crop silage (3-03-590 Pea, silage)

	ME	DOMD	Dig NDF	Dig CP	Eff N Dg	ODM	TDM	GE	CP
Mean	**7.7**	**545**	**–**	**0.59**	**A**	**253**	**276**	**17.8**	**179**
Min	6.5	449	–	0.48		174	193	15.0	124
Max	8.8	635	–	0.66		303	320	20.0	222
SD	0.92	77.8	–	0.07		48.0	50.3	1.9	47.1
n	4	4	–	5		5	5	5	5

[1]ME and DOMD per kg TDM; digestibility values as coefficients; effective N degradability as a coefficient at a fractional outflow rate of 0.05 per hour - where coefficients have not been determined, the degradability group (A to D; see Glossary of Terms, page 3) is indicated.

[2]DM as ODM and TDM per kg FW; GE per kg TDM; other values per kg ODM.

Chemical composition[2]

EE	AEE	NDF	ADF	Lignin	WSC	Starch	NCD	TA	Ca	P	Mg
g	g	g	g	g	g	g	g	g	g	g	g
27	–	**505**	**290**	–	–	–	–	**56**	–	–	–
15	–	392	238	–	–	–	–	39	–	–	–
36	–	634	365	–	–	–	–	92	–	–	–
6.2	–	88.3	47.9	–	–	–	–	15.3	–	–	–
11	–	10	10	–	–	–	–	11	–	–	–
32	–	**446**	**261**	–	–	–	–	**52**	–	–	–
15	–	376	217	–	–	–	–	41	–	–	–
39	–	680	378	–	–	–	–	86	–	–	–
5.9	–	84.5	47.1	–	–	–	–	12.6	–	–	–
12	–	12	12	–	–	–	–	12	–	–	–
35	–	**280**	**239**	**89**	**72**	**6**	**698**	**143**	**12.6**	**3.0**	**2.2**
19	–	280	239	77	2	0	698	72	7.8	2.3	1.5
49	–	280	239	108	322	13	698	218	18.5	3.8	3.2
11.7	–	–	–	16.4	140.2	6.6	–	64.1	3.8	0.68	0.73
5	–	1	1	3	5	3	1	5	5	5	5

FEED CLASS 40

ENERGY FEEDS

Nutritive values[1]

	ME	DOMD	Dig NDF	Dig CP	Eff N Dg	DM	GE	CP
	MJ	g				g	MJ	g

Apples, fresh (4-00-421 Apple, fruit, fresh)

	ME	DOMD	Dig NDF	Dig CP	Eff N Dg	DM	GE	CP
Mean	11.9	856	–	0.24	A	136	16.8	38
Min	11.1	824	–	0.24		126	16.8	33
Max	12.7	889	–	0.24		145	16.8	44
SD	1.2	46.1	–	–		13.5	0.0	8.1
n	2	2	–	–		2	2	2

Apple pomace (4-00-424 Apple, pomace, wet)

	ME	DOMD	Dig NDF	Dig CP	Eff N Dg	DM	GE	CP
Mean	9.1	608	–	0.24	B	242	19.8	69
Min	8.6	497	–	0.09		204	19.0	64
Max	9.9	683	–	0.39		282	21.8	79
SD	0.50	72.0	–	0.21		32.8	1.2	8.7
n	5	5	–	2		5	5	3

Barley grain, all seasons (4-00-549 Barley, grain)

	ME	DOMD	Dig NDF	Dig CP	Eff N Dg	DM	GE	CP
Mean	13.3	838	0.57	0.77	0.85	864	18.5	129
Min	12.1	569	0.42	0.66	0.83	792	18.0	100
Max	14.3	874	0.80	0.84	0.87	910	18.9	171
SD	0.50	53.2	0.09	0.04	0.014	19.4	0.19	14.6
n	45	30	25	45	13	65	65	65

Barley grain, spring (4-25-097 Barley, spring, grain)

	ME	DOMD	Dig NDF	Dig CP	Eff N Dg	DM	GE	CP
Mean	13.2	852	0.58	0.77	0.86	869	18.5	128
Min	12.1	837	0.42	0.66	0.83	825	18.0	100
Max	13.9	871	0.80	0.84	0.87	888	18.8	171
SD	0.49	11.4	0.09	0.04	0.013	11.2	0.20	14.8
n	32	16	16	32	9	40	40	40

Barley grain, winter (4-00-569 Barley, winter, grain)

	ME	DOMD	Dig NDF	Dig CP	Eff N Dg	DM	GE	CP
Mean	13.5	842	0.56	0.77	0.84	857	18.5	130
Min	12.7	813	0.43	0.73	0.83	792	18.2	101
Max	14.2	874	0.69	0.81	0.85	910	18.9	160
SD	0.48	21.0	0.09	0.02	0.082	26.2	0.16	15.6
n	8	8	8	8	4	20	20	20

[1]ME and DOMD per kg DM; digestibility values as coefficients; effective N degradability as a coefficient at a fractional outflow rate of 0.05 per hour - where coefficients have not been determined, the degradability group (A to D; see Glossary of Terms, page 3) is indicated.

[2]DM as ODM per kg FW; other values per kg DM.

Chemical composition[2]

EE	AEE	NDF	ADF	Lignin	WSC	Sugars	Starch	NCD	TA	Ca	P	Mg
g	g	g	g	g	g	g	g	g	g	g	g	g
12	**–**	**126**	**117**	**23**	**726**	**–**	**2**	**–**	**20**	**0.5**	**0.9**	**0.3**
10	–	117	105	23	719	–	2	–	18	0.3	0.8	0.2
14	–	135	129	23	732	–	3	–	22	0.7	1.0	0.3
2.8	–	12.7	17.0	–	9.2	–	0.8	–	2.8	0.28	0.14	0.07
2	–	2	2	1	2	–	2	–	2	2	2	2
27	**29**	**489**	**415**	**172**	**161**	**–**	**30**	**769**	**18**	**1.6**	**1.4**	**0.6**
23	20	425	355	166	93	–	2	751	15	0.9	1.3	0.4
32	33	540	522	178	228	–	78	783	22	2.4	1.6	0.7
3.8	5.8	53.4	72.4	8.5	95.5	–	35.2	16.4	3.1	0.61	0.13	0.12
5	4	5	5	2	2	–	5	4	5	5	5	5
16	**26**	**201**	**64**	**17**	**37**	**17**	**562**	**887**	**26**	**0.9**	**4.0**	**1.2**
5	14	133	43	7	30	8	257	851	20	0.1	3.0	0.8
40	33	366	91	31	44	30	636	913	52	3.3	5.5	2.1
5.5	6.6	47.8	10.7	5.4	9.9	7.0	65.3	13.5	6.3	0.58	0.46	0.20
65	50	63	55	52	2	12	56	40	65	56	57	54
15	**25**	**207**	**65**	**17**	**–**	**29**	**572**	**889**	**27**	**0.7**	**4.0**	**1.1**
5	14	133	50	10	–	27	516	868	20	0.1	3.0	0.8
25	32	275	86	26	–	30	636	913	50	1.4	5.0	1.3
5.1	7.0	40.1	9.7	4.3	–	2.1	30.2	13.3	6.1	0.25	0.4	0.14
40	24	38	32	32	–	2	34	16	40	34	34	31
18	**28**	**178**	**61**	**16**	**–**	**14**	**585**	**886**	**24**	**0.8**	**3.9**	**1.2**
14	14	140	43	7	–	8	504	851	21	0.4	3.1	1.0
23	33	242	91	31	–	21	625	904	32	2.1	4.6	1.6
2.6	5.1	31.9	12.3	7.0	–	4.6	33.8	14.2	2.8	0.36	0.37	0.15
20	20	20	18	18	–	10	18	18	20	18	18	18

Nutritive values[1]

	ME	DOMD	Dig NDF	Dig CP	Eff N Dg		DM	GE	CP
	MJ	g					g	MJ	g

Cassava meal (4-09-598 Cassava, common, tubers, dehydrated)

Mean	12.6	852	–	–	B		885	16.8	28
Min	12.1	821	–	–			884	16.6	26
Max	12.9	930	–	–			887	17.1	29
SD	0.42	44.8	–	–			2.4	0.19	1.5
n	5	5	–	–			2	5	5

Citrus pulp, dried (4-01-237 Citrus, pomace without fines,

Mean	12.6	825	0.86	0.56	B		890	17.5	68
Min	11.3	771	0.83	0.44			875	17.3	53
Max	14.2	875	0.91	0.63			913	17.9	79
SD	0.87	35.3	0.04	0.06			9.5	0.15	6.4
n	8	8	3	8			13	13	13

Coffee residue, dried (4-06-651 Coffee, instant beverage

Mean	–	–	–	–	D		901	25.2	116
Min	–	–	–	–			856	24.3	110
Max	–	–	–	–			942	25.9	124
SD	–	–	–	–			31.3	0.60	5.3
n	–	–	–	–			5	5	5

Coffee residue, fresh (1-01-576 Coffee, grounds, wet)

Mean	10.0	572	–	–	D		315	25.2	107
Min	10.0	572	–	–			315	25.2	107
Max	10.0	572	–	–			315	25.2	107
SD	–	–	–	–			–	–	–
n	1	1	–	–			1	1	1

Fodder beet, fresh (4-00-637 Beet, mangel, roots, fresh)

Mean	11.9	829	0.74	0.51	A		183	16.0	63
Min	11.6	802	0.60	0.36			159	15.6	51
Max	12.4	854	0.84	0.62			214	16.6	80
SD	0.29	17.7	0.11	0.07			18.6	0.37	9.5
n	10	10	4	10			10	10	10

[1]ME and DOMD per kg DM; digestibility values as coefficients; effective N degradability as a coefficient at a fractional outflow rate of 0.05 per hour - where coefficients have not been determined, the degradability group (A to D; see Glossary of Terms, page 3) is indicated.

[2]DM as ODM per kg FW; other values per kg DM.

Chemical composition[2]

EE	AEE	NDF	ADF	Lignin	WSC	Sugars	Starch	NCD	TA	Ca	P	Mg
g	g	g	g	g	g	g	g	g	g	g	g	g
4	**6**	**114**	**63**	**13**	**47**	**–**	**645**	**900**	**50**	**2.2**	**0.9**	**1.4**
2	5	48	37	5	33	–	527	893	22	1.8	0.7	1.1
7	7	275	76	20	70	–	755	906	62	3.3	1.0	2.4
1.8	1.4	91.5	22.5	7.6	19.9	–	94.8	9.2	16.1	0.63	0.14	0.57
5	2	5	3	3	3	–	5	2	5	5	5	5

dehydrated)

EE	AEE	NDF	ADF	Lignin	WSC	Sugars	Starch	NCD	TA	Ca	P	Mg
22	**22**	**228**	**202**	**39**	**248**	**250**	**2**	**904**	**63**	**14.6**	**1.1**	**1.7**
16	14	185	130	7	182	241	0	870	59	10.7	1.0	1.0
40	33	290	266	116	291	277	5	916	73	18.8	1.2	2.6
6.2	6.1	36.8	54.2	38.6	33.7	14.9	2.1	12.1	4.3	2.4	0.09	0.50
13	10	13	13	13	7	5	6	13	13	13	13	13

residue, dehydrated)

EE	AEE	NDF	ADF	Lignin	WSC	Sugars	Starch	NCD	TA	Ca	P	Mg
255	**266**	**–**	**–**	**–**	**–**	**4**	**3**	**559**	**19**	**2.3**	**0.4**	**0.3**
219	237	–	–	–	–	1	0	506	4	1.0	0.2	0.1
273	279	–	–	–	–	5	8	607	74	6.4	1.0	0.6
20.5	16.3	–	–	–	–	1.7	3.9	36.5	31.0	2.3	0.36	0.20
5	5	–	–	–	–	4	5	5	5	5	5	5

EE	AEE	NDF	ADF	Lignin	WSC	Sugars	Starch	NCD	TA	Ca	P	Mg
211	**199**	**740**	**696**	**30**	**–**	**–**	**11**	**452**	**6**	**1.0**	**0.1**	**0.2**
211	199	740	696	30	–	–	11	452	6	1.0	0.1	0.2
211	199	740	696	30	–	–	11	452	6	1.0	0.1	0.2
–	–	–	–	–	–	–	–	–	–	–	–	–
1	1	1	1	1	–	–	1	1	1	1	1	1

EE	AEE	NDF	ADF	Lignin	WSC	Sugars	Starch	NCD	TA	Ca	P	Mg
3	**4**	**136**	**72**	**21**	**660**	**–**	**1**	**874**	**81**	**2.8**	**1.8**	**1.6**
1	3	105	54	12	547	–	0	848	50	0.8	1.5	1.1
4	5	172	84	29	819	–	5	905	105	9.1	2.4	2.1
1.2	1.1	22.6	10.1	7.5	75.5	–	1.9	23.6	19.9	2.4	0.27	0.30
10	4	10	10	4	10	–	7	4	10	10	10	10

Nutritive values[1]

	ME	DOMD	Dig NDF	Dig CP	Eff N Dg	DM	GE	CP
	MJ	g				g	MJ	g

Grape juice concentrate (4-08-569 Grape, syrup)

	ME	DOMD	Dig NDF	Dig CP	Eff N Dg	DM	GE	CP
Mean	13.4	930	–	–	–	599	16.0	–
Min	13.4	930	–	–	–	599	16.0	–
Max	13.4	930	–	–	–	599	16.0	–
SD	–	–	–	–	–	–	–	–
n	1	1	–	–	–	1	1	–

Maize fibre (4-07-113 Maize, starch process residue, wet)

	ME	DOMD	Dig NDF	Dig CP	Eff N Dg	DM	GE	CP
Mean	13.4	787	0.78	0.73	B	378	19.9	147
Min	12.2	770	0.75	0.66		344	18.5	111
Max	14.5	811	0.80	0.79		416	20.7	212
SD	0.85	15.4	0.02	0.06		28.3	0.85	38.5
n	5	5	5	5		5	5	5

Maize gluten feed (4-25-384 Maize, starch process residue,

	ME	DOMD	Dig NDF	Dig CP	Eff N Dg	DM	GE	CP
Mean	12.9	765	0.76	0.77	0.84	885	19.1	220
Min	11.3	690	0.59	0.66	0.83	856	18.5	201
Max	14.2	864	0.88	0.84	0.86	908	20.2	252
SD	0.65	40.7	0.08	0.05	0.014	13.0	0.46	12.1
n	22	22	14	22	5	28	28	28

Maize grain (4-02-879 Maize grain *and* 4-02-859 Maize, grain,

	ME	DOMD	Dig NDF	Dig CP	Eff N Dg	DM	GE	CP
Mean	13.8	879	–	–	B	873	18.9	102
Min	12.7	816	–	–		855	18.6	83
Max	14.9	930	–	–		890	19.1	118
SD	0.53	31.1	–	–		12.7	0.10	6.6
n	16	16	–	–		12	28	28

Naked oats grain, all seasons (4-25-101 Oats, hull-less, grain)

	ME	DOMD	Dig NDF	Dig CP	Eff N Dg	DM	GE	CP
Mean	14.8	857	0.54	0.78	0.94	865	20.0	128
Min	14.1	784	0.35	0.71	0.92	801	19.5	103
Max	15.3	910	0.73	0.83	0.95	889	20.4	164
SD	0.36	35.9	0.17	0.04	0.015	27.1	0.26	17.1
n	10	10	4	10	3	15	15	15

[1]ME and DOMD per kg DM; digestibility values as coefficients; effective N degradability as a coefficient at a fractional outflow rate of 0.05 per hour - where coefficients have not been determined, the degradability group (A to D; see Glossary of Terms, page 3) is indicated.

[2]DM as ODM per kg FW; other values per kg DM.

Chemical composition[(2)]

EE	AEE	NDF	ADF	Lignin	WSC	Sugars	Starch	NCD	TA	Ca	P	Mg
g	g	g	g	g	g	g	g	g	g	g	g	g
2	–	–	–	–	–	–	–	–	15	–	–	–
2	–	–	–	–	–	–	–	–	15	–	–	–
2	–	–	–	–	–	–	–	–	15	–	–	–
–	–	–	–	–	–	–	–	–	–	–	–	–
1	–	–	–	–	–	–	–	–	1	–	–	–
31	**42**	**538**	**154**	**27**	**15**	**–**	**181**	**616**	**22**	**0.3**	**3.3**	**1.4**
24	35	362	120	18	7	–	101	566	9	0.1	1.0	0.5
44	49	597	176	40	25	–	255	671	72	0.5	11.0	4.7
8.0	5.9	100.7	21.3	8.9	7.7	–	55.8	47.1	28.1	0.17	4.3	1.8
5	4	5	5	5	4	–	5	4	5	5	5	5

dehydrated)

EE	AEE	NDF	ADF	Lignin	WSC	Sugars	Starch	NCD	TA	Ca	P	Mg
44	**51**	**383**	**114**	**21**	**24**	**21**	**186**	**724**	**72**	**2.3**	**9.3**	**4.1**
17	29	327	81	9	18	11	91	687	34	0.1	6.4	2.4
80	81	451	147	41	38	31	283	800	95	10.8	11.6	5.3
17.3	16.1	36.7	17.4	10.0	9.3	7.4	53.7	25.0	15.3	3.6	1.2	0.70
28	28	28	28	25	4	5	26	28	28	27	28	28

flaked)

EE	AEE	NDF	ADF	Lignin	WSC	Sugars	Starch	NCD	TA	Ca	P	Mg
39	**42**	**117**	**28**	**6**	**–**	**18**	**700**	**927**	**15**	**0.1**	**3.0**	**1.3**
22	31	91	19	2	–	10	661	924	11	0.1	2.5	1.0
51	52	176	38	12	–	27	755	931	21	0.5	3.9	1.6
6.5	6.5	22.9	5.5	2.9	–	6.5	26.1	2.9	2.2	0.11	0.32	0.13
28	11	25	21	21	–	8	24	5	28	17	24	21

EE	AEE	NDF	ADF	Lignin	WSC	Sugars	Starch	NCD	TA	Ca	P	Mg
90	**101**	**114**	**42**	**16**	**23**	**8**	**590**	**932**	**22**	**0.7**	**4.2**	**1.3**
71	65	59	20	9	14	7	537	872	18	0.4	3.1	1.1
100	113	164	76	32	33	9	653	959	27	0.9	4.9	1.5
8.2	11.8	32.8	17.9	5.9	7.0	0.81	36.9	26.9	2.8	0.16	0.52	0.12
15	14	15	15	14	5	5	15	14	15	15	15	15

Nutritive values[1]

	ME	DOMD	Dig NDF	Dig CP	Eff N Dg	DM	GE	CP
	MJ	g				g	MJ	g

Naked oats grain, spring (4-25-101 Oats, hull-less, grain, spring)

	ME	DOMD	Dig NDF	Dig CP	Eff N Dg	DM	GE	CP
Mean	**14.8**	**848**	**0.63**	**0.78**	**0.94**	**860**	**20.1**	**123**
Min	14.1	784	0.63	0.71	0.92	801	19.5	103
Max	15.3	898	0.63	0.83	0.95	883	20.4	164
SD	0.43	37.1	–	0.04	0.015	28.0	0.26	15.7
n	7	7	1	7	3	12	12	12

Naked oats grain, winter (4-25-101 Oats, hull-less, grain, winter)

	ME	DOMD	Dig NDF	Dig CP	Eff N Dg	DM	GE	CP
Mean	**14.9**	**878**	**0.51**	**0.80**	**A**	**886**	**19.9**	**147**
Min	14.7	861	0.35	0.76		879	19.7	145
Max	15.0	910	0.73	0.82		889	20.1	150
SD	0.15	27.6	0.20	0.03		5.5	0.20	2.1
n	3	3	3	3		3	3	3

Oats grain, all seasons (4-03-309 Oats, grain)

	ME	DOMD	Dig NDF	Dig CP	Eff N Dg	DM	GE	CP
Mean	**12.1**	**740**	**0.40**	**0.73**	**0.93**	**858**	**19.6**	**108**
Min	10.6	659	0.23	0.66	0.90	820	19.1	79
Max	13.4	792	0.52	0.77	0.94	894	20.2	149
SD	0.77	54	0.14	0.04	0.019	18.9	0.22	14.5
n	21	5	5	5	4	29	29	29

Oats grain, spring (4-03-309 Oats, grain, spring)

	ME	DOMD	Dig NDF	Dig CP	Eff N Dg	DM	GE	CP
Mean	**11.9**	**–**	**–**	**–**	**–**	**854**	**19.6**	**108**
Min	10.6	–	–	–	–	820	19.1	79
Max	13.4	–	–	–	–	894	20.2	149
SD	0.72	–	–	–	–	18.3	0.23	15.8
n	15	–	–	–	–	23	23	23

Oats grain, winter (4-03-309 Oats, grain, winter)

	ME	DOMD	Dig NDF	Dig CP	Eff N Dg	DM	GE	CP
Mean	**12.5**	**740**	**0.40**	**0.73**	**0.93**	**874**	**19.5**	**108**
Min	11.1	659	0.23	0.66	0.90	851	19.3	99
Max	13.4	792	0.52	0.77	0.94	889	19.7	121
SD	0.81	54.0	0.14	0.04	0.019	12.6	0.18	8.2
n	6	5	5	5	4	6	6	6

[1]ME and DOMD per kg DM; digestibility values as coefficients; effective N degradability as a coefficient at a fractional outflow rate of 0.05 per hour - where coefficients have not been determined, the degradability group (A to D; see Glossary of Terms, page 3) is indicated.

[2]DM as ODM per kg FW; other values per kg DM.

Chemical composition[2]

EE	AEE	NDF	ADF	Lignin	WSC	Sugars	Starch	NCD	TA	Ca	P	Mg
g	g	g	g	g	g	g	g	g	g	g	g	g
92	**101**	**123**	**44**	**16**	**23**	**8**	**581**	**925**	**22**	**0.7**	**4.1**	**1.3**
71	65	91	20	9	14	7	537	872	18	0.4	3.1	1.1
100	113	164	76	26	33	9	637	958	27	0.9	4.8	1.5
8.4	13.2	27.6	18.5	4.2	7.0	0.8	34.4	26.0	3.1	0.14	0.52	0.13
12	11	12	12	11	5	5	12	11	12	12	12	12
84	**100**	**76**	**32**	**20**	–	–	**625**	**958**	**21**	**0.6**	**4.6**	**1.2**
81	93	59	23	12	–	–	604	957	20	0.4	4.2	1.1
87	105	107	48	32	–	–	653	959	22	0.8	4.9	1.3
3.0	6.4	26.6	13.7	10.8	–	–	25.3	1.1	1.2	0.21	0.36	0.12
3	3	3	3	3	–	–	3	3	3	3	3	3
41	**58**	**310**	**149**	**37**	–	**11**	**471**	**763**	**27**	**0.9**	**3.4**	**3.0**
16	29	255	129	27	–	8	420	713	22	0.5	2.4	0.8
72	80	364	177	55	–	21	530	819	38	1.2	4.0	13.3
16.0	17.5	27.8	13.1	7.7	–	5.1	26.9	31.5	3.4	0.18	0.46	4.2
29	13	28	26	26	–	6	27	10	29	27	27	26
37	**51**	**315**	**152**	**37**	–	**11**	**469**	**755**	**27**	**0.9**	**3.4**	**3.6**
16	29	255	129	27	–	8	420	730	22	0.5	3.0	0.8
72	80	364	177	55	–	21	530	784	38	1.2	4.0	13.3
14.7	18.5	27.6	13.4	7.5	–	5.1	26.8	20.2	3.6	0.19	0.45	4.7
23	8	22	20	20	–	6	21	5	23	21	20	20
56	**70**	**292**	**142**	**39**	–	–	**478**	**771**	**26**	**0.8**	**3.3**	**1.0**
33	63	256	131	29	–	–	436	713	23	0.6	2.4	0.9
67	75	312	153	54	–	–	517	819	30	0.9	4.0	1.1
12.4	5.4	22.7	8.8	8.8	–	–	28.1	40.7	2.5	0.15	0.54	0.06
6	5	6	6	6	–	–	6	5	6	6	6	6

Nutritive values[1]

	ME	DOMD	Dig NDF	Dig CP	Eff N Dg	DM	GE	CP
	MJ	g				g	MJ	g

Olive pulp meal (4-03-413 Olive, fruit without pits, meal

Mean	4.3	199	–	–	C	881	20.0	108
Min	4.3	199	–	–		881	20.0	108
Max	4.3	199	–	–		881	20.0	108
SD	–	–	–	–		–	–	–
n	1	1	–	–		1	1	1

Pectin extracted fruits (Apple and citrus pulp, pectin extracted

Mean	9.9	603	–	0.23	–	164	20.7	105
Min	9.3	582	–	0.19	–	154	20.1	104
Max	10.5	625	–	0.28	–	173	21.2	106
SD	0.80	30.6	–	0.06	–	13.4	0.78	1.4
n	2	2	–	2	–	2	2	2

Potatoes, fresh (4-03-787 Potato, tubers, fresh)

Mean	13.4	882	–	–	A	204	17.2	108
Min	13.3	882	–	–		199	17.2	103
Max	13.4	882	–	–		209	17.3	113
SD	0.02	–	–	–		7.2	0.09	7.0
n	2	1	–	–		2	2	2

Potato, processing waste (4-03-775 Potato, process residue,

Mean	10.5	634	–	0.49	A	983	16.5	91
Min	10.5	634	–	0.49		983	16.5	91
Max	10.5	634	–	0.49		983	16.5	91
SD	–	–	–	–		–	–	–
n	1	1	–	1		1	1	1

Rice bran meal, expelled (4-13-293 Rice, bran with germs, meal

Mean	11.0	585	–	0.65	C	902	18.9	128
Min	11.0	585	–	0.65		902	18.9	128
Max	11.0	585	–	0.65		902	18.9	128
SD	–	–	–	–		–	–	–
n	1	1	–	1		1	1	1

[1]ME and DOMD per kg DM; digestibility values as coefficients; effective N degradability as a coefficient at a fractional outflow rate of 0.05 per hour - where coefficients have not been determined, the degradability group (A to D; see Glossary of Terms, page 3) is indicated.

[2]DM as ODM per kg FW; other values per kg DM.

Chemical composition[(2)]

EE	AEE	NDF	ADF	Lignin	WSC	Sugars	Starch	NCD	TA	Ca	P	Mg
g	g	g	g	g	g	g	g	g	g	g	g	g

mechanical extracted)

| 18 | 16 | 684 | 543 | 240 | 16 | – | 3 | 337 | 76 | 15.1 | 1.1 | 1.2 |

18	16	684	543	240	16	–	3	337	76	15.1	1.1	1.2
18	16	684	543	240	16	–	3	337	76	15.1	1.1	1.2
–	–	–	–	–	–	–	–	–	–	–	–	–
1	1	1	1	1	1	–	1	1	1	1	1	1

residue)

| 36 | 42 | 767 | 708 | 197 | 9 | – | 8 | 704 | 13 | 2.7 | 1.4 | 0.1 |

35	40	764	705	175	6	–	8	688	10	1.5	1.4	0.1
36	43	770	711	218	12	–	8	719	16	3.8	1.4	0.1
0.71	2.1	4.2	4.2	30.4	4.2	–	–	21.9	4.2	1.6	0.00	0.00
2	2	2	2	2	2	–	1	2	2	2	2	2

| 2 | – | 73 | 44 | 14 | 73 | – | 565 | – | 53 | 0.4 | 2.0 | 1.0 |

2	–	71	43	14	60	–	550	–	51	0.3	1.9	1.0
3	–	76	45	14	87	–	580	–	54	0.4	2.0	1.0
0.1	–	3.6	1.2	0.2	19.4	–	21.5	–	2.2	0.07	0.07	0.00
2	–	2	2	2	2	–	2	–	2	2	2	2

dehydrated)

| 22 | – | – | – | 5 | 132 | – | 452 | – | 92 | 0.6 | 1.8 | 0.5 |

22	–	–	–	5	132	–	452	–	92	0.6	1.8	0.5
22	–	–	–	5	132	–	452	–	92	0.6	1.8	0.5
–	–	–	–	–	–	–	–	–	–	–	–	–
1	–	–	–	1	1	–	1	–	1	1	1	1

mechanical extracted)

| 90 | – | 370 | 242 | 58 | 24 | – | 302 | 660 | 113 | 0.9 | 11.0 | 4.5 |

90	–	370	242	58	24	–	302	660	113	0.9	11.0	4.5
90	–	370	242	58	24	–	302	660	113	0.9	11.0	4.5
–	–	–	–	–	–	–	–	–	–	–	–	–
1	–	1	1	1	1	–	1	1	1	1	1	1

Nutritive values[1]

	ME	DOMD	Dig NDF	Dig CP	Eff N Dg		DM	GE	CP
	MJ	g					g	MJ	g

Rice bran meal, extracted (4-03-930 Rice, bran with germs, meal

Mean	7.1	461	–	0.60	C		896	16.7	154
Min	6.7	427	–	0.55			875	16.5	139
Max	7.3	478	–	0.65			909	17.0	171
SD	0.32	29.2	–	0.05			10.7	0.18	11.0
n	3	3	–	3			8	8	8

Rye grain (4-04-047 Rye, grain)

Mean	–	–	–	–	A		869	18.5	119
Min	–	–	–	–			865	18.2	106
Max	–	–	–	–			872	18.8	133
SD	–	–	–	–			5.0	0.38	19.0
n	–	–	–	–			2	2	2

Sainfoin, low temperature dried (Sainfoin dehydrated at low

Mean	10.9	652	–	0.51	B		854	20.0	189
Min	10.9	652	–	0.51			854	20.0	189
Max	10.9	652	–	0.51			854	20.0	189
SD	–	–	–	–			–	–	–
n	1	1	–	1			1	1	1

Sorghum grain (4-04-383 Sorghum, grain)

Mean	13.2	850	–	–	A		897	18.7	113
Min	12.1	807	–	–			897	18.5	106
Max	14.4	895	–	–			897	18.9	129
SD	0.99	38.5	–	–			–	0.15	9.3
n	4	4	–	–			1	5	5

Sugar beet feed, dried, molassed (4-00-672 Beet, sugar, pulp

Mean	12.5	823	0.92	0.71	B		876	17.0	110
Min	11.7	798	0.90	0.67			831	16.5	97
Max	13.1	846	0.93	0.75			907	17.4	139
SD	0.36	12.3	0.01	0.03			16.7	0.25	8.7
n	14	14	3	6			58	19	66

[1]ME and DOMD per kg DM; digestibility values as coefficients; effective N degradability as a coefficient at a fractional outflow rate of 0.05 per hour - where coefficients have not been determined, the degradability group (A to D; see Glossary of Terms, page 3) is indicated.

[2]DM as ODM per kg FW; other values per kg DM.

Chemical composition[(2)]

EE	AEE	NDF	ADF	Lignin	WSC	Sugars	Starch	NCD	TA	Ca	P	Mg
g	g	g	g	g	g	g	g	g	g	g	g	g

solvent extracted)

7	**18**	**451**	**275**	**70**	**30**	**19**	**236**	**543**	**70**	**0.9**	**17.4**	**3.8**
5	15	401	242	56	22	12	172	459	15	0.2	14.9	0.7
10	21	561	340	100	43	24	302	589	170	2.2	19.9	8.9
1.6	2.4	54.4	32.2	14.6	11.2	4.4	44.9	41.9	74.8	0.96	1.7	4.1
8	5	8	8	8	3	5	8	8	8	8	8	8

12	**29**	**357**	–	–	–	–	–	–	**18**	–	–	–
11	29	351	–	–	–	–	–	–	18	–	–	–
13	29	364	–	–	–	–	–	–	18	–	–	–
1.4	0.1	9.1	–	–	–	–	–	–	0.6	–	–	–
2	2	2	–	–	–	–	–	–	2	–	–	–

temperature)

19	**17**	**448**	–	–	–	–	**5**	**701**	**78**	**13.7**	**3.0**	**2.1**
19	17	448	–	–	–	–	5	701	78	13.7	3.0	2.1
19	17	448	–	–	–	–	5	701	78	13.7	3.0	2.1
–	–	–	–	–	–	–	–	–	–	–	–	–
1	1	1	–	–	–	–	1	1	1	1	1	1

30	–	**107**	**57**	**24**	–	**15**	**730**	–	**17**	**0.3**	**2.8**	**1.1**
22	–	105	49	18	–	15	690	–	16	0.2	2.2	1.0
35	–	110	71	34	–	15	761	–	19	0.8	3.2	1.3
5.2	–	2.2	10.2	7.3	–	–	30.8	–	1.2	0.27	0.48	0.13
5	–	4	4	4	–	1	5	–	5	5	5	4

with molasses, dehydrated)

4	**4**	**321**	**179**	**23**	**281**	**235**	**65**	**860**	**88**	**7.6**	**0.8**	**1.1**
3	3	271	164	15	251	212	0	826	75	5.0	0.6	0.8
8	6	377	190	36	317	249	137	877	110	12.4	1.1	1.6
1.3	1.2	29.2	7.9	5.7	20.7	14.6	59.6	14.1	9.3	2.0	0.15	0.19
19	11	19	19	19	14	5	10	11	19	19	19	19

Nutritive values[1]

	ME	DOMD	Dig NDF	Dig CP	Eff N Dg		DM	GE	CP
	MJ	g					g	MJ	g

Sugar beet feed, dried, unmolassed (4-00-669 Beet, sugar, pulp,

	ME	DOMD	Dig NDF	Dig CP	Eff N Dg		DM	GE	CP
Mean	**12.9**	**832**	**0.86**	**0.54**	**B**		**856**	**17.1**	**77**
Min	12.6	822	0.86	0.54			826	16.6	77
Max	13.2	840	0.86	0.54			902	17.6	77
SD	0.28	9.5	–	–			40.1	0.50	–
n	3	3	1	1			3	3	1

Sugar beet feed, ensiled (4-00-662 Beet, sugar, pulp, silage)

	ME	DOMD	Dig NDF	Dig CP	Eff N Dg		DM	GE	CP
Mean	**11.5**	**757**	**–**	**0.59**	**B**		**163**	**17.0**	**111**
Min	10.5	725	–	0.42			142	16.0	104
Max	12.3	817	–	0.75			178	17.7	119
SD	0.84	42.4	–	0.14			15.9	0.78	6.3
n	4	4	–	4			4	4	4

Sugar beet feed, molassed, ensiled (Beet, sugar, pulp with

	ME	DOMD	Dig NDF	Dig CP	Eff N Dg		DM	GE	CP
Mean	**–**	**–**	**–**	**–**	**–**		**213**	**17.6**	**131**
Min	–	–	–	–	–		209	17.5	127
Max	–	–	–	–	–		216	17.8	140
SD	–	–	–	–	–		3.8	0.15	7.3
n	–	–	–	–	–		3	3	3

Sugar beet feed, pressed (4-08-582 Beet, sugar, pulp, pressed)

	ME	DOMD	Dig NDF	Dig CP	Eff N Dg		DM	GE	CP
Mean	**11.7**	**761**	**–**	**0.48**	**B**		**256**	**17.0**	**98**
Min	10.6	708	–	0.45			165	16.6	81
Max	12.5	799	–	0.51			333	17.3	123
SD	0.86	40.3	–	0.04			21.5	0.28	4.4
n	5	5	–	2			363	5	274

Sugar beet feed, pressed, molassed (4-06-938 Beet, sugar, pulp

	ME	DOMD	Dig NDF	Dig CP	Eff N Dg		DM	GE	CP
Mean	**–**	**–**	**–**	**–**	**–**		**322**	**17.1**	**104**
Min	–	–	–	–	–		276	17.1	101
Max	–	–	–	–	–		352	17.1	112
SD	–	–	–	–	–		15.9	–	2.5
n	–	–	–	–	–		51	1	16

[1]ME and DOMD per kg DM; digestibility values as coefficients; effective N degradability as a coefficient at a fractional outflow rate of 0.05 per hour - where coefficients have not been determined, the degradability group (A to D; see Glossary of Terms, page 3) is indicated.

[2]DM as ODM per kg FW; other values per kg DM.

Chemical composition[2]

EE	AEE	NDF	ADF	Lignin	WSC	Sugars	Starch	NCD	TA	Ca	P	Mg
g	g	g	g	g	g	g	g	g	g	g	g	g
dehydrated)												
7	**5**	**372**	**213**	**38**	**79**	**–**	**3**	**884**	**68**	**7.6**	**0.8**	**1.8**
5	4	304	170	36	79	–	3	881	46	6.9	0.7	1.2
10	6	501	282	41	79	–	3	886	89	8.2	0.8	2.8
2.9	1.4	111.5	60.6	2.6	–	–	–	3.5	21.5	0.65	0.06	0.85
3	2	3	3	3	1	–	1	2	3	3	3	3
7	**10**	**418**	**273**	**30**	**36**	**–**	**2**	**855**	**93**	**10.2**	**1.2**	**1.9**
2	7	384	257	23	16	–	0	845	72	7.4	1.1	1.8
10	13	458	285	35	64	–	3	872	127	16.0	1.3	2.0
3.4	3.1	35.7	11.7	5.2	20.6	–	1.1	14.6	24.1	4.0	0.11	0.10
4	3	4	4	4	4	–	4	3	4	4	4	4
molasses, silage)												
6	**10**	**341**	**202**	**50**	**22**	**–**	**tr**	**846**	**96**	**7.7**	**0.8**	**1.5**
5	10	333	199	34	16	–	tr	824	84	6.9	0.6	1.3
7	10	348	205	59	29	–	tr	878	105	8.4	1.1	1.8
1.0	–	10.6	4.2	13.9	6.4	–	–	28.4	10.7	0.76	0.25	0.27
3	1	2	2	3	3	–	1	3	3	3	3	3
6	**5**	**523**	**251**	**29**	**45**	**–**	**4**	**804**	**82**	**10.3**	**1.2**	**1.9**
5	5	489	243	22	29	–	1	743	65	7.6	1.0	1.4
6	5	590	258	35	64	–	6	850	110	12.5	1.3	2.3
0.6	0.0	45.5	6.3	5.0	12.7	–	2.7	44.1	17.1	1.8	0.13	0.34
5	4	4	4	5	5	–	3	5	5	5	5	5
with molasses, pressed)												
2	**8**	**–**	**–**	**14**	**–**	**–**	**7**	**904**	**69**	**4.9**	**0.8**	**1.6**
2	8	–	–	14	–	–	7	904	69	4.9	0.8	1.6
2	8	–	–	14	–	–	7	904	69	4.9	0.8	1.6
–	–	–	–	–	–	–	–	–	–	–	–	–
1	1	–	–	1	–	–	1	1	1	1	1	1

Nutritive values[1]

	ME	DOMD	Dig NDF	Dig CP	Eff N Dg	DM	GE	CP
	MJ	g				g	MJ	g

Swedes (4-04-001 *Ruta baga (Brassica napus)*, roots, fresh)

Mean	14.0	876	–	–	A	105	17.3	91
Min	13.9	871	–	–		95	17.3	85
Max	14.0	882	–	–		114	17.4	96
SD	0.08	7.8	–	–		13.1	0.07	8.1
n	2	2	–	–		2	2	2

Triticale grain, winter (4-20-362 Triticale, grain, winter)

Mean	13.8	878	0.77	0.79	0.90	864	18.3	138
Min	12.8	847	0.54	0.72	0.89	845	17.7	102
Max	15.2	907	0.95	0.86	0.90	891	18.6	173
SD	0.76	21.0	0.21	0.05	0.071	15.1	0.26	20.8
n	9	9	3	9	2	14	14	14

Wheat bran (4-05-190 Wheat, bran)

Mean	10.8	698	–	–	B	892	18.9	174
Min	10.2	651	–	–		874	18.7	141
Max	11.7	761	–	–		906	19.2	197
SD	0.65	46.0	–	–		11.3	0.13	15.0
n	4	4	–	–		10	10	10

Wheat feed (4-06-749 Wheat, flour by-product, less than 12%

Mean	11.9	731	0.54	0.75	A	890	19.1	179
Min	11.2	665	0.50	0.74		861	18.7	159
Max	14.3	830	0.56	0.77		918	19.3	197
SD	1.0	47.8	0.03	0.01		18.0	0.19	12.8
n	8	8	4	4		13	13	13

Wheat grain, all seasons (4-05-211 Wheat, grain)

Mean	13.7	889	0.60	0.77	0.90	857	18.4	128
Min	12.3	850	0.47	0.66	0.87	789	17.9	97
Max	14.7	923	0.80	0.87	0.94	888	19.0	161
SD	0.62	20.6	0.12	0.05	0.025	21.2	0.23	16.5
n	26	26	10	26	7	45	45	45

[1]ME and DOMD per kg DM; digestibility values as coefficients; effective N degradability as a coefficient at a fractional outflow rate of 0.05 per hour - where coefficients have not been determined, the degradability group (A to D; see Glossary of Terms, page 3) is indicated.

[2]DM as ODM per kg FW; other values per kg DM.

Chemical composition[2]

EE	AEE	NDF	ADF	Lignin	WSC	Sugars	Starch	NCD	TA	Ca	P	Mg
g	g	g	g	g	g	g	g	g	g	g	g	g
4	**–**	**140**	**125**	**14**	**587**	**–**	**–**	**–**	**60**	**3.5**	**2.6**	**1.1**
4	–	139	121	14	578	–	–	–	54	3.4	2.4	1.0
4	–	142	130	14	596	–	–	–	66	3.5	2.8	1.1
0.3	–	1.6	6.5	0.4	12.7	–	–	–	8.0	0.07	0.28	0.07
2	–	2	2	2	2	–	–	–	2	2	2	2
16	**22**	**119**	**36**	**11**	**51**	**32**	**517**	**917**	**21**	**0.5**	**4.3**	**1.2**
12	18	83	27	8	44	31	379	904	18	0.3	3.7	1.0
19	25	147	44	14	70	34	688	933	25	0.7	4.8	1.4
1.8	2.4	18.0	5.4	2.1	10.9	1.2	97.2	9.8	1.7	0.16	0.41	0.14
14	14	14	14	13	5	5	14	10	14	14	14	14
39	**52**	**475**	**137**	**40**	**–**	**64**	**196**	**685**	**66**	**1.1**	**12.6**	**6.2**
33	47	403	111	31	–	51	116	634	56	0.7	7.3	4.3
53	55	550	173	49	–	72	269	728	73	1.3	15.2	12.0
6.8	3.2	54.7	20.5	6.1	–	7.5	49.2	38.7	5.4	0.18	3.0	2.7
10	5	9	9	9	–	6	10	5	10	10	10	9

fibre)

EE	AEE	NDF	ADF	Lignin	WSC	Sugars	Starch	NCD	TA	Ca	P	Mg
43	**51**	**364**	**111**	**35**	**84**	**57**	**277**	**748**	**51**	**1.1**	**10.5**	**5.2**
31	44	243	61	23	74	50	148	730	34	0.9	6.8	3.3
73	55	435	138	49	89	65	449	771	58	1.4	15.3	10.7
10.6	3.2	53.6	18.2	8.6	7.0	6.1	75.2	15.2	6.0	0.14	2.0	2.6
13	9	13	13	13	4	5	13	9	13	13	13	13
17	**21**	**124**	**30**	**11**	**–**	**27**	**674**	**928**	**17**	**0.6**	**3.3**	**1.1**
12	16	92	23	8	–	5	615	913	12	0.2	2.6	0.80
30	26	175	40	16	–	38	768	936	22	1.1	4.4	1.3
3.4	2.5	21.1	4.3	2.3	–	9.5	33.1	6.3	2.2	0.21	0.42	0.13
45	29	44	36	36	–	11	37	20	45	37	37	36

Nutritive values[1]

	ME	DOMD	Dig NDF	Dig CP	Eff N Dg	DM	GE	CP
	MJ	g				g	MJ	g

Wheat grain, spring (4-25-107 Wheat, spring, grain)

	ME	DOMD	Dig NDF	Dig CP	Eff N Dg	DM	GE	CP
Mean	13.4	890	–	0.79	–	864	18.8	146
Min	13.4	890	–	0.79	–	857	18.5	137
Max	13.4	890	–	0.79	–	871	19.0	155
SD	–	–	–	–	–	9.9	0.38	12.7
n	1	1	–	1	–	2	2	2

Wheat grain, winter (4-28-312 Wheat, winter, grain)

	ME	DOMD	Dig NDF	Dig CP	Eff N Dg	DM	GE	CP
Mean	13.7	889	0.60	0.77	0.90	857	18.4	127
Min	12.3	850	0.47	0.66	0.87	789	17.9	97
Max	14.7	923	0.80	0.87	0.94	888	19.0	161
SD	0.62	21.0	0.12	0.05	0.025	21.6	0.21	16.2
n	25	25	10	25	7	43	43	43

Wheat middlings (4-05-205 Wheat, flour by-product, less than

	ME	DOMD	Dig NDF	Dig CP	Eff N Dg	DM	GE	CP
Mean	–	–	–	–	–	879	19.2	175
Min	–	–	–	–	–	879	19.2	175
Max	–	–	–	–	–	879	19.2	175
SD	–	–	–	–	–	–	–	–
n	–	–	–	–	–	1	1	1

Wheat offals (4-06-749 Wheat, flour by-product, less than 12%

	ME	DOMD	Dig NDF	Dig CP	Eff N Dg	DM	GE	CP
Mean	11.9	732	–	–	B	878	19.1	185
Min	10.6	691	–	–		864	18.8	163
Max	13.9	843	–	–		886	19.3	211
SD	0.95	48.1	–	–		6.3	0.15	17.4
n	8	8	–	–		8	8	8

[1]ME and DOMD per kg DM; digestibility values as coefficients; effective N degradability as a coefficient at a fractional outflow rate of 0.05 per hour - where coefficients have not been determined, the degradability group (A to D; see Glossary of Terms, page 3) is indicated.

[2]DM as ODM per kg FW; other values per kg DM.

Chemical composition[2]

EE	AEE	NDF	ADF	Lignin	WSC	Sugars	Starch	NCD	TA	Ca	P	Mg
g	g	g	g	g	g	g	g	g	g	g	g	g
24	**21**	**145**	**36**	**12**	–	–	**625**	–	**18**	**0.5**	**3.9**	**1.2**
18	21	134	36	12	–	–	625	–	17	0.5	3.9	1.2
30	21	156	36	12	–	–	625	–	19	0.5	3.9	1.2
8.4	–	15.5	–	–	–	–	–	–	1.6	–	–	–
2	1	2	1	1	–	–	1	–	2	1	1	1
17	**22**	**123**	**30**	**11**	–	**27**	**676**	**928**	**17**	**0.6**	**3.3**	**1.1**
12	16	92	23	8	–	5	615	913	12	0.2	2.6	0.8
23	26	175	40	16	–	38	768	936	22	1.1	4.4	1.3
2.9	2.6	21.0	4.2	2.3	–	9.5	32.5	6.3	2.2	0.21	0.42	0.13
43	28	42	35	35	–	11	36	20	43	36	36	35

9.5% fibre)

EE	AEE	NDF	ADF	Lignin	WSC	Sugars	Starch	NCD	TA	Ca	P	Mg
39	**37**	–	–	–	–	**65**	**306**	–	**48**	**1.4**	**10.6**	–
39	37	–	–	–	–	65	306	–	48	1.4	10.6	–
39	37	–	–	–	–	65	306	–	48	1.4	10.6	–
–	–	–	–	–	–	–	–	–	–	–	–	–
1	1	–	–	–	–	1	1	–	1	1	1	–

fibre)

EE	AEE	NDF	ADF	Lignin	WSC	Sugars	Starch	NCD	TA	Ca	P	Mg
47	–	**354**	**104**	**36**	–	–	**329**	–	**51**	**1.0**	**11.9**	**8.7**
41	–	238	58	23	–	–	157	–	31	0.8	10.3	5.9
59	–	505	147	42	–	–	500	–	71	1.2	13.8	11.5
5.9	–	81.7	26.9	6.1	–	–	108	–	11.6	0.11	1.2	1.8
8	–	8	8	8	–	–	8	–	8	8	8	8

FEED CLASS 50

PROTEIN SUPPLEMENTS

Nutritive values[1]

	ME	DOMD	Dig NDF	Dig CP	Eff N Dg		DM	GE	CP
	MJ	g					g	MJ	g

Beans, field, spring (Bean, field, seeds, spring; *Vicia faba*)

Mean	13.4	872	0.48	0.84	0.84		861	18.6	330
Min	12.5	813	0.48	0.84	0.84		857	18.2	265
Max	14.5	896	0.48	0.84	0.84		865	18.8	369
SD	0.65	26.9	–	–	–		5.7	0.17	33.5
n	9	9	1	1	1		2	10	10

Beans, field, winter (Bean, field, seeds, winter; *Vicia faba*)

Mean	13.1	880	0.58	0.82	–		848	18.4	267
Min	12.5	826	0.57	0.81	–		842	17.9	253
Max	13.6	929	0.59	0.82	–		854	18.6	283
SD	0.45	40.3	0.02	0.00	–		8.7	0.25	11.7
n	6	6	2	2	–		2	6	6

Blood meal (5-00-380 Animal, blood, meal)

Mean	–	–	–	–	–		915	24.5	905
Min	–	–	–	–	–		895	24.2	901
Max	–	–	–	–	–		938	24.9	908
SD	–	–	–	–	–		16.7	0.25	3.2
n	–	–	–	–	–		5	5	5

Brewers grains (5-00-517 Barley, brewers grains, wet)

Mean	11.5	589	–	0.77	B		250	21.3	218
Min	10.7	543	–	0.73			120	20.7	172
Max	12.2	628	–	0.81			338	21.9	327
SD	0.65	34.4	–	0.03			31.3	0.35	34.2
n	6	6	–	6			92	20	64

Copra, expelled (5-01-572 Coconut, kernels with coats, meal

Mean	12.9	669	–	0.77	B		934	21.3	198
Min	12.5	599	–	0.73			894	19.2	154
Max	13.3	739	–	0.82			956	24.6	233
SD	0.51	99.0	–	0.06			26.7	2.0	29.6
n	2	2	–	2			6	6	6

[1]ME and DOMD per kg DM; digestibility values as coefficients; effective N degradability as a coefficient at a fractional outflow rate of 0.05 per hour - where coefficients have not been determined, the degradability group (A to D; see Glossary of Terms, page 3) is indicated.

[2]DM as ODM per kg FW; other values per kg DM.

Chemical composition[2]

EE	AEE	NDF	ADF	Lignin	WSC	Sugars	Starch	NCD	TA	Ca	P	Mg
g	g	g	g	g	g	g	g	g	g	g	g	g
13	**16**	**186**	**123**	**15**	**–**	**47**	**365**	**940**	**37**	**1.1**	**5.2**	**1.8**
8	16	118	110	11	–	47	335	940	32	0.8	3.8	1.2
22	16	210	138	19	–	47	424	940	42	1.6	6.1	2.2
4.3	–	27.8	9.5	2.7	–	–	27.7	–	3.1	0.23	0.67	0.29
10	1	9	8	8	–	1	10	1	10	10	10	9
13	**18**	**167**	**124**	**18**	**–**	**–**	**395**	**920**	**35**	**1.3**	**8.6**	**1.9**
10	18	130	118	12	–	–	315	908	30	1.0	5.9	1.3
16	18	186	127	26	–	–	433	931	43	1.9	10.8	2.3
2.2	0.0	21.8	4.3	6.5	–	–	41.3	16.3	4.3	0.33	2.1	0.43
5	2	6	4	4	–	–	6	2	6	6	6	6
–	**12**	**–**	**–**	**–**	**–**	**–**	**–**	**–**	**20**	**0.6**	**1.5**	**0.2**
–	9	–	–	–	–	–	–	–	18	0.1	1.3	0.2
–	14	–	–	–	–	–	–	–	21	0.7	1.7	0.2
–	2.2	–	–	–	–	–	–	–	1.0	0.26	0.19	0.0
–	5	–	–	–	–	–	–	–	5	5	5	5
62	**55**	**618**	**264**	**86**	**13**	**–**	**38**	**591**	**38**	**3.5**	**5.1**	**1.7**
32	46	499	216	47	4	–	7	492	4	1.1	2.7	1.1
99	71	753	315	172	27	–	96	647	56	6.2	7.5	2.5
16.7	13.7	63.9	26.6	36.5	6.1	–	24.4	35.8	6.0	1.4	1.0	0.36
64	3	17	17	19	18	–	15	19	64	20	20	20

mechanical extracted)

EE	AEE	NDF	ADF	Lignin	WSC	Sugars	Starch	NCD	TA	Ca	P	Mg
168	**–**	**517**	**281**	**65**	**–**	**114**	**2**	**696**	**52**	**0.6**	**5.4**	**3.0**
72	–	502	273	59	–	86	2	684	43	0.4	5.3	2.8
333	–	532	289	71	–	142	2	707	63	0.7	5.4	3.1
96.4	–	21.2	11.3	8.5	–	39.6	0.0	16.3	8.9	0.21	0.07	0.21
6	–	2	2	2	–	2	2	2	6	2	2	2

Nutritive values[1]

	ME	DOMD	Dig NDF	Dig CP	Eff N Dg	DM	GE	CP
	MJ	g				g	MJ	g

Cottonseed meal (5-30-144 Cotton, seeds with some hulls,

Mean	11.1	627	0.49	0.77	0.66	944	20.6	379
Min	9.3	540	0.39	0.75	0.66	902	20.2	356
Max	12.9	716	0.62	0.82	0.66	976	20.9	401
SD	1.5	72.1	0.11	0.03	–	22.8	0.24	17.3
n	4	4	4	4	1	9	9	9

Distillers dark grains, barley based (5-12-185 Barley, distillers

Mean	12.2	612	–	–	C	907	21.3	275
Min	12.1	612	–	–		880	20.9	251
Max	12.4	612	–	–		930	21.7	289
SD	0.18	0.0	–	–			20.9	0.26	13.1
n	2	2	–	–		7	7	7

Distillers dark grains, maize based (5-02-843 Maize, distillers

Mean	14.7	726	0.81	0.78	0.57	889	22.4	317
Min	13.6	636	0.77	0.77	0.55	858	21.7	261
Max	15.4	791	0.85	0.80	0.59	930	23.7	437
SD	0.85	61.1	0.06	0.02	0.03	27.7	0.79	70.1
n	5	5	2	2	2	5	5	5

Distillers dark grains, wheat based (5-05-194 Wheat, distillers

Mean	12.4	699	0.59	0.61	0.92	890	21.5	302
Min	12.2	663	0.43	0.53	0.82	845	20.7	265
Max	12.8	736	0.72	0.68	0.97	933	22.6	336
SD	0.28	33.3	0.12	0.06	0.058	32.8	0.65	25.5
n	5	5	5	5	5	10	10	10

Draff, barley based (5-00-519 Barley, distillers grains, wet)

Mean	10.2	500	–	0.74	C	248	21.5	211
Min	9.5	482	–	0.73		243	21.4	207
Max	10.8	517	–	0.75		253	21.6	214
SD	0.92	24.7	–	0.01		7.1	0.14	5.0
n	2	2	–	2		2	2	2

[1]ME and DOMD per kg DM; digestibility values as coefficients; effective N degradability as a coefficient at a fractional outflow rate of 0.05 per hour - where coefficients have not been determined, the degradability group (A to D ; see Glossary of Terms, page 3) is indicated.

[2]DM as ODM per kg FW; other values per kg DM.

Chemical composition[(2)]

EE	AEE	NDF	ADF	Lignin	WSC	Sugars	Starch	NCD	TA	Ca	P	Mg
g	g	g	g	g	g	g	g	g	g	g	g	g

mechanical extracted (expeller), caked)

EE	AEE	NDF	ADF	Lignin	WSC	Sugars	Starch	NCD	TA	Ca	P	Mg
64	**67**	**385**	**245**	**62**	**68**	**51**	**17**	**750**	**61**	**2.1**	**8.9**	**5.8**
56	60	330	193	48	67	46	8	686	54	1.7	6.5	5.1
72	74	467	303	86	69	54	32	785	66	2.4	10.3	6.4
5.8	3.9	49.6	34.9	15.6	1.0	2.8	7.7	29.1	4.2	0.21	1.1	0.43
9	9	9	9	9	3	5	8	9	9	9	9	9

grains with solubles, dehydrated)

EE	AEE	NDF	ADF	Lignin	WSC	Sugars	Starch	NCD	TA	Ca	P	Mg
67	**85**	**420**	**175**	**32**	**18**	**39**	**26**	**687**	**60**	**1.7**	**9.6**	**3.3**
53	73	404	165	30	17	23	14	671	56	1.4	8.3	2.7
74	92	435	184	34	19	66	34	721	69	2.2	10.6	3.8
7.8	7.8	21.9	13.4	2.8	1.4	18.0	8.4	19.8	4.2	0.32	0.80	0.34
7	5	2	2	2	2	5	7	5	7	7	7	7

grains with solubles, dehydrated)

EE	AEE	NDF	ADF	Lignin	WSC	Sugars	Starch	NCD	TA	Ca	P	Mg
110	**109**	**343**	**216**	**92**	**50**	**–**	**24**	**823**	**46**	**1.4**	**8.4**	**3.2**
90	108	232	151	50	6	–	14	816	20	0.40	4.2	0.6
130	109	261	261	134	108	–	43	829	58	2.1	10.5	4.5
18.6	0.71	83.0	55.7	39.9	44.5	–	11.4	9.2	15.7	0.65	2.5	1.5
5	2	5	5	5	5	–	5	2	5	5	5	5

grains with solubles, dehydrated)

EE	AEE	NDF	ADF	Lignin	WSC	Sugars	Starch	NCD	TA	Ca	P	Mg
55	**69**	**335**	**193**	**85**	**86**	**63**	**45**	**822**	**52**	**1.8**	**8.8**	**2.8**
32	42	230	119	32	55	50	26	773	42	1.0	7.4	2.1
92	103	462	275	157	132	70	69	884	73	2.8	11.0	3.4
20.6	17.4	91.2	58	50.2	33.3	8.1	19.8	42.6	10.3	0.62	1.1	0.44
10	10	10	10	10	5	5	5	10	10	0	10	0

EE	AEE	NDF	ADF	Lignin	WSC	Sugars	Starch	NCD	TA	Ca	P	Mg
86	**–**	**673**	**294**	**63**	**5**	**–**	**18**	**–**	**34**	**1.5**	**3.8**	**1.8**
84	–	656	264	58	4	–	14	–	33	1.5	3.8	1.8
88	–	689	324	68	6	–	21	–	35	1.5	3.8	1.8
2.8	–	23.3	42.4	7.1	1.4	–	5.0	–	1.4	–	–	–
2	–	2	2	2	2	–	2	–	2	1	1	1

Nutritive values[1]

	ME	DOMD	Dig NDF	Dig CP	Eff N Dg	DM	GE	CP
	MJ	g				g	MJ	g

Feather meal (5-03-795 Poultry, feathers meal hydrolysed)

	ME	DOMD	Dig NDF	Dig CP	Eff N Dg	DM	GE	CP
Mean	–	–	–	–	–	907	24.0	892
Min	–	–	–	–	–	885	23.9	889
Max	–	–	–	–	–	915	24.1	895
SD	–	–	–	–	–	12.3	0.08	2.1
n	–	–	–	–	–	5	5	5

Fishmeal, Chilean (5-24-017 Fish, meal, mechanical extracted,

	ME	DOMD	Dig NDF	Dig CP	Eff N Dg	DM	GE	CP
Mean	14.9	792	–	0.91	D	911	20.7	709
Min	14.4	777	–	0.89		893	19.6	631
Max	15.6	821	–	0.93		959	21.5	736
SD	0.54	19.7	–	0.02		18.4	0.56	29.9
n	4	4	–	4		10	10	10

Fishmeal, herring (5-02-000 Fish, herring, meal, mechanical

	ME	DOMD	Dig NDF	Dig CP	Eff N Dg	DM	GE	CP
Mean	16.4	805	–	0.96	D	913	22.0	758
Min	14.9	773	–	0.94		889	20.7	714
Max	17.8	837	–	0.97		939	23.1	824
SD	2.0	45.2	–	0.02		16.5	0.78	31.1
n	2	2	–	2		10	10	10

Fishmeal, mixed meal (Fish, meal, various sources)

	ME	DOMD	Dig NDF	Dig CP	Eff N Dg	DM	GE	CP
Mean	15.2	762	–	0.93	D	932	19.7	701
Min	15.1	738	–	0.91		930	19.4	686
Max	15.3	779	–	0.95		932	20.0	710
SD	0.11	21.8	–	0.02		0.92	0.30	12.9
n	3	3	–	3		3	3	3

Fishmeal, offal meal white (Fish, meal, various from white fish)

	ME	DOMD	Dig NDF	Dig CP	Eff N Dg	DM	GE	CP
Mean	13.4	737	–	0.93	D	914	20.2	716
Min	12.1	708	–	0.91		893	19.7	706
Max	14.5	789	–	0.94		938	20.9	728
SD	1.2	45.2	–	0.02		18.3	0.49	9.3
n	3	3	–	3		4	4	4

[1]ME and DOMD per kg DM; digestibility values as coefficients; effective N degradability as a coefficient at a fractional outflow rate of 0.05 per hour - where coefficients have not been determined, the degradability group (A to D ; see Glossary of Terms, page 3) is indicated.

[2]DM as ODM per kg FW; other values per kg DM.

Chemical composition[2]

EE	AEE	NDF	ADF	Lignin	WSC	Sugars	Starch	NCD	TA	Ca	P	Mg
g	g	g	g	g	g	g	g	g	g	g	g	g
64	**80**	–	–	–	–	**2**	–	–	**25**	**5.6**	**3.1**	**0.4**
63	79	–	–	–	–	1	–	–	25	5.5	3.1	0.3
64	81	–	–	–	–	3	–	–	26	5.7	3.2	0.4
0.73	0.63	–	–	–	–	0.9	–	–	0.3	0.07	0.06	0.04
5	5	–	–	–	–	3	–	–	5	5	5	5

more than 70% protein, 3.1-8% fat; Chilean origin)

EE	AEE	NDF	ADF	Lignin	WSC	Sugars	Starch	NCD	TA	Ca	P	Mg
88	**103**	–	–	–	–	–	–	**825**	**169**	**42.8**	**27.4**	**2.5**
64	91	–	–	–	–	–	–	808	150	33.3	23.4	2.1
104	118	–	–	–	–	–	–	837	194	55.3	33.8	2.7
13.6	8.7	–	–	–	–	–	–	14.9	12.4	8.4	3.5	0.19
10	7	–	–	–	–	–	–	3	10	8	8	8

extracted)

EE	AEE	NDF	ADF	Lignin	WSC	Sugars	Starch	NCD	TA	Ca	P	Mg
95	**73**	–	–	–	**4**	–	–	**869**	**139**	**34.4**	**23.6**	**2.1**
64	73	–	–	–	4	–	–	869	112	31.3	22.3	2.1
137	73	–	–	–	4	–	–	869	178	39.5	26.0	2.2
23.7	–	–	–	–	–	–	–	–	24.5	4.5	2.1	0.06
10	1	–	–	–	1	–	–	1	10	3	3	2

EE	AEE	NDF	ADF	Lignin	WSC	Sugars	Starch	NCD	TA	Ca	P	Mg
89	**86**	–	–	–	–	–	–	**777**	**214**	**65.3**	**37.3**	**2.0**
68	78	–	–	–	–	–	–	760	202	60.0	36.0	2.0
126	101	–	–	–	–	–	–	796	222	70.0	38.0	2.1
32.1	13.0	–	–	–	–	–	–	18.1	10.4	5.0	1.2	0.06
3	3	–	–	–	–	–	–	3	3	3	3	3

EE	AEE	NDF	ADF	Lignin	WSC	Sugars	Starch	NCD	TA	Ca	P	Mg
80	**90**	–	–	–	–	–	–	**781**	**208**	**57.2**	**33.2**	**2.0**
71	84	–	–	–	–	–	–	776	192	46.9	27.8	1.9
95	94	–	–	–	–	–	–	784	214	63.4	36.2	2.1
10.8	5.3	–	–	–	–	–	–	4.6	10.6	9.0	4.7	0.11
4	3	–	–	–	–	–	–	3	4	3	3	3

Nutritive values[1]

	ME	DOMD	Dig NDF	Dig CP	Eff N Dg	DM	GE	CP
	MJ	g				g	MJ	g

Fishmeal, Peruvian (5-24-018 Fish, meal, mechanical extracted,

	ME	DOMD	Dig NDF	Dig CP	Eff N Dg	DM	GE	CP
Mean	–	–	–	–	D	889	22.0	709
Min	–	–	–	–		889	22.0	709
Max	–	–	–	–		889	22.0	709
SD	–	–	–	–		–	–	–
n	–	–	–	–		1	1	1

Fishmeal, white (Fish, meal, various from white fish)

	ME	DOMD	Dig NDF	Dig CP	Eff N Dg	DM	GE	CP
Mean	14.2	751	–	0.92	0.46	911	19.7	693
Min	12.1	683	–	0.90	0.46	888	18.5	672
Max	17.0	803	–	0.94	0.46	955	21.0	738
SD	1.7	44.2	–	0.02	–	21.5	0.79	21.4
n	6	6	–	6	1	8	8	8

Groundnut meal (5-03-648 Peanut, seeds without coats,

	ME	DOMD	Dig NDF	Dig CP	Eff N Dg	DM	GE	CP
Mean	13.7	772	–	–	A	925	20.6	512
Min	13.3	756	–	–		925	20.2	476
Max	14.2	788	–	–		925	20.9	547
SD	0.61	22.6	–	–		–	0.34	35.3
n	2	2	–	–		1	3	3

Linseed meal (5-02-043 Flax, common, seeds, mechanical

	ME	DOMD	Dig NDF	Dig CP	Eff N Dg	DM	GE	CP
Mean	–	–	–	–	–	885	24.2	391
Min	–	–	–	–	–	884	24.2	387
Max	–	–	–	–	–	886	24.4	395
SD	–	–	–	–	–	1.0	0.09	3.4
n	–	–	–	–	–	5	5	5

Maize germ meal (5-07-146 Maize, germs, meal mechanical

	ME	DOMD	Dig NDF	Dig CP	Eff N Dg	DM	GE	CP
Mean	14.5	764	–	–	–	879	19.7	108
Min	13.1	733	–	–	–	874	19.2	98
Max	15.8	794	–	–	–	888	20.5	119
SD	1.5	33.8	–	–	–	6.3	0.54	8.0
n	4	4	–	–	–	5	9	9

[1]ME and DOMD per kg DM; digestibility values as coefficients; effective N degradability as a coefficient at a fractional outflow rate of 0.05 per hour - where coefficients have not been determined, the degradability group (A to D; see Glossary of Terms, page 3) is indicated.

[2]DM as ODM per kg FW; other values per kg DM.

Chemical composition[2]

EE	AEE	NDF	ADF	Lignin	WSC	Sugars	Starch	NCD	TA	Ca	P	Mg
g	g	g	g	g	g	g	g	g	g	g	g	g

more than 70% protein, more than 8% fat, Peruvian origin)

EE	AEE	NDF	ADF	Lignin	WSC	Sugars	Starch	NCD	TA	Ca	P	Mg
122	–	–	–	–	–	–	–	–	**190**	–	–	–
122	–	–	–	–	–	–	–	–	190	–	–	–
122	–	–	–	–	–	–	–	–	190	–	–	–
–	–	–	–	–	–	–	–	–	–	–	–	–
1	–	–	–	–	–	–	–	–	1	–	–	–

EE	AEE	NDF	ADF	Lignin	WSC	Sugars	Starch	NCD	TA	Ca	P	Mg
75	**87**	–	–	–	**5**	–	–	**796**	**213**	**56.2**	**38.1**	**2.3**
52	72	–	–	–	4	–	–	770	169	46.0	28.6	1.7
98	107	–	–	–	6	–	–	830	266	64.7	70.1	2.5
17.9	15.3	–	–	–	1.2	–	–	26.4	28.9	6.0	14.5	0.31
8	5	–	–	–	3	–	–	4	8	7	7	6

mechanical extracted, caked)

EE	AEE	NDF	ADF	Lignin	WSC	Sugars	Starch	NCD	TA	Ca	P	Mg
70	–	**180**	**146**	**41**	**95**	**77**	**53**	–	**69**	**2.0**	**6.2**	**3.5**
61	–	148	143	34	92	77	47	–	58	0.9	6.0	3.3
79	–	212	148	47	97	77	58	–	85	4.0	6.4	3.6
9.0	–	45.2	3.5	9.2	3.5	–	7.8	–	14.3	1.7	0.20	0.21
3	–	2	2	2	2	1	2	–	3	3	3	2

extracted, caked)

EE	AEE	NDF	ADF	Lignin	WSC	Sugars	Starch	NCD	TA	Ca	P	Mg
87	**96**	**192**	**131**	**16**	–	**42**	**52**	**856**	**51**	**3.4**	**8.7**	**5.4**
85	94	183	124	9	–	41	50	852	51	3.4	8.6	5.3
90	99	206	140	26	–	43	54	861	51	3.5	8.8	5.5
2.0	2.0	8.6	6.0	7.8	–	0.7	1.3	3.1	0.0	0.05	0.08	0.09
5	5	5	5	5	–	5	5	5	5	5	5	5

extracted)

EE	AEE	NDF	ADF	Lignin	WSC	Sugars	Starch	NCD	TA	Ca	P	Mg
82	**64**	**224**	**60**	**16**	**43**	**16**	**532**	**852**	**25**	**0.2**	**5.2**	**2.1**
54	60	178	49	10	37	12	368	838	19	0.1	3.7	1.5
129	68	319	80	26	46	19	624	859	37	0.2	8.3	3.3
30.4	2.9	47.1	11.5	5.8	4.4	2.5	107.5	8.3	6.9	0.04	1.6	0.69
9	5	9	9	9	4	5	9	5	9	9	9	9

Nutritive values[1]

	ME	DOMD	Dig NDF	Dig CP	Eff N Dg	DM	GE	CP
	MJ	g				g	MJ	g

Maize gluten meal (5-09-318 Maize, gluten, meal, 60% protein)

	ME	DOMD	Dig NDF	Dig CP	Eff N Dg	DM	GE	CP
Mean	17.5	944	0.93	0.95	0.38	904	23.7	669
Min	17.0	911	0.93	0.94	0.30	883	22.9	616
Max	18.2	991	0.93	0.97	0.45	923	24.9	729
SD	0.41	30.7	–	0.02	0.106	12.4	0.61	33.9
n	5	5	1	5	2	10	10	10

Malt culms (5-00-545 Barley, malt sprouts, dehydrated)

	ME	DOMD	Dig NDF	Dig CP	Eff N Dg	DM	GE	CP
Mean	–	–	–	–	–	915	18.7	283
Min	–	–	–	–	–	889	18.2	247
Max	–	–	–	–	–	965	19.0	320
SD	–	–	–	–	–	28.9	0.35	26.4
n	–	–	–	–	–	5	5	5

Meat and bone meal (5-00-388 Animal, meat with bone, meal

	ME	DOMD	Dig NDF	Dig CP	Eff N Dg	DM	GE	CP
Mean	12.3	664	–	0.86	C	960	18.3	534
Min	11.0	621	–	0.84		912	15.2	514
Max	13.7	707	–	0.88		973	19.9	603
SD	1.9	60.8	–	0.03		22.6	1.3	23.4
n	2	2	–	2		13	13	13

Palm kernel meal (5-03-487 Palm (*Elaeis* spp), kernels with coats,

	ME	DOMD	Dig NDF	Dig CP	Eff N Dg	DM	GE	CP
Mean	11.6	646	0.62	0.75	0.52	895	20.4	170
Min	9.5	486	0.44	0.59	0.47	852	19.6	140
Max	13.0	751	0.77	0.83	0.60	918	20.9	193
SD	1.3	94.2	0.12	0.08	0.070	23.2	0.44	22.4
n	7	7	7	7	3	7	7	7

Peas, field (5-03-600 Pea, seeds)

	ME	DOMD	Dig NDF	Dig CP	Eff N Dg	DM	GE	CP
Mean	13.5	909	–	0.89	B	866	18.5	254
Min	12.7	886	–	0.89		843	17.9	226
Max	14.4	932	–	0.89		884	18.7	284
SD	0.58	15.2	–	0.0		15.5	0.23	15.7
n	6	6	–	2		7	11	11

[1]ME and DOMD per kg DM; digestibility values as coefficients; effective N degradability as a coefficient at a fractional outflow rate of 0.05 per hour - where coefficients have not been determined, the degradability group (A to D; see Glossary of Terms, page 3) is indicated.

[2]DM as ODM per kg FW; other values per kg DM.

Chemical composition[2]

EE	AEE	NDF	ADF	Lignin	WSC	Sugars	Starch	NCD	TA	Ca	P	Mg
g	g	g	g	g	g	g	g	g	g	g	g	g
29	**69**	**84**	**105**	**28**	**6**	**3**	**155**	**984**	**11**	**0.6**	**2.8**	**0.5**
15	48	12	2	0	3	2	81	975	7	0.1	1.5	0.3
53	100	246	255	108	7	4	245	991	21	4.0	5.0	0.9
12.2	17.8	93.4	108.3	37.3	1.7	0.8	54.6	5.8	4.3	1.3	1.2	0.25
10	7	8	10	9	4	5	10	7	10	9	10	10
14	**26**	**463**	**163**	**11**	**–**	**107**	**63**	**381**	**65**	**2.7**	**7.4**	**2.0**
10	21	426	126	5	–	65	26	364	62	1.3	6.4	1.6
17	32	511	188	15	–	184	122	400	68	3.9	8.8	2.5
3.2	4.2	34.9	23.3	3.5	–	47.9	36.0	17.6	2.4	1.0	0.90	0.34
5	5	5	5	5	–	5	5	5	5	5	5	5

rendered)

EE	AEE	NDF	ADF	Lignin	WSC	Sugars	Starch	NCD	TA	Ca	P	Mg
128	**151**	**–**	**–**	**–**	**–**	**4**	**–**	**–**	**284**	**89.9**	**42.6**	**2.2**
8	139	–	–	–	–	3	–	–	250	57.0	27.8	1.6
175	165	–	–	–	–	5	–	–	332	113.4	56.0	2.3
47.2	11.8	–	–	–	–	0.9	–	–	22.8	13.0	6.5	0.18
13	10	–	–	–	–	5	–	–	13	13	13	12

meal mechanical extracted)

EE	AEE	NDF	ADF	Lignin	WSC	Sugars	Starch	NCD	TA	Ca	P	Mg
83	**76**	**693**	**470**	**68**	**39**	**–**	**12**	**447**	**44**	**2.4**	**6.2**	**3.0**
69	58	637	428	54	39	–	0	388	39	2.1	5.4	2.4
96	87	731	518	84	39	–	26	496	50	2.9	6.9	3.4
8.2	10.3	39.0	38.1	11.6	–	–	11.7	41.8	3.3	0.27	0.61	0.41
7	6	7	7	7	1	–	6	7	7	7	7	7
14	**25**	**116**	**76**	**8**	**75**	**57**	**440**	**957**	**30**	**1.0**	**5.8**	**1.6**
11	22	94	61	1	73	46	374	944	26	0.7	4.0	1.1
20	26	173	105	20	77	65	519	962	35	1.4	9.4	2.3
2.6	2.1	22.1	13.1	6.0	2.8	7.3	44.4	6.3	2.9	0.21	2.1	0.44
11	5	11	11	11	2	5	11	7	11	11	11	11

Nutritive values[1]

	ME	DOMD	Dig NDF	Dig CP	Eff N Dg	DM	GE	CP
	MJ	g				g	MJ	g

Pot ale syrup (5-12-210 Barley, distillers solubles, condensed)

Mean	15.4	805	–	0.78	B	483	20.0	374
Min	15.4	805	–	0.78		483	20.0	374
Max	15.4	805	–	0.78		483	20.0	374
SD	–	–	–	–		–	–	–
n	1	1	–	1		1	1	1

Poultry offal meal (5-24-876 Poultry, by-product, dehydrated,

Mean	–	–	–	–	–	905	26.8	545
Min	–	–	–	–	–	896	25.8	497
Max	–	–	–	–	–	922	27.8	584
SD	–	–	–	–	–	10.4	0.86	31.6
n	–	–	–	–	–	5	5	5

Rapeseed meal (5-03-871 Rape, seeds, meal solvent extracted)

Mean	12.0	708	0.53	0.84	0.78	899	19.7	402
Min	10.6	621	0.35	0.76	0.68	882	19.1	351
Max	13.2	768	0.73	0.95	0.84	929	20.5	432
SD	0.83	41.8	0.15	0.05	0.057	13.3	0.35	19.0
n	12	12	7	12	6	17	17	17

Sesame cake (5-11-533 Sesame, seeds, mechanical extracted,

Mean	–	–	–	–	–	952	19.9	488
Min	–	–	–	–	–	950	19.8	476
Max	–	–	–	–	–	954	20.0	499
SD	–	–	–	–	–	2.1	0.10	7.9
n	–	–	–	–	–	5	5	5

Soyabean meal, extracted (5-04-604 Soybean, seeds, meal solvent

Mean	13.3	844	–	–	B	886	19.5	493
Min	12.6	800	–	–		875	19.1	400
Max	14.0	877	–	–		902	19.9	531
SD	0.54	32.6	–	–		10.3	0.25	32.8
n	6	6	–	–		9	15	15

[1]ME and DOMD per kg DM; digestibility values as coefficients; effective N degradability as a coefficient at a fractional outflow rate of 0.05 per hour - where coefficients have not been determined, the degradability group (A to D; see Glossary of Terms, page 3) is indicated.

[2]DM as ODM per kg FW; other values per kg DM.

Chemical composition[2]

EE	AEE	NDF	ADF	Lignin	WSC	Sugars	Starch	NCD	TA	Ca	P	Mg
g	g	g	g	g	g	g	g	g	g	g	g	g
2	–	**6**	–	**15**	**23**	–	**13**	–	**95**	**1.9**	**20.1**	**6.4**
2	–	6	–	15	23	–	13	–	95	1.9	20.1	6.4
2	–	6	–	15	23	–	13	–	95	1.9	20.1	6.4
–	–	–	–	–	–	–	–	–	–	–	–	–
1	–	1	–	1	1	–	1	–	1	1	1	1

viscera with feet with heads)

EE	AEE	NDF	ADF	Lignin	WSC	Sugars	Starch	NCD	TA	Ca	P	Mg
347	**355**	–	–	–	–	**3**	–	**558**	**73**	**19.0**	**9.7**	**0.7**
323	331	–	–	–	–	2	–	499	49	12.9	8.1	0.5
407	412	–	–	–	–	4	–	588	90	23.5	13.3	0.9
34.2	32.5	–	–	–	–	1.1	–	35.3	17.9	5.4	2.1	0.16
5	5	–	–	–	–	5	–	5	5	5	5	5

EE	AEE	NDF	ADF	Lignin	WSC	Sugars	Starch	NCD	TA	Ca	P	Mg
34	**54**	**295**	**206**	**53**	**103**	**107**	**40**	**766**	**76**	**8.4**	**11.3**	**4.4**
7	25	247	167	26	90	105	4	724	67	5.1	7.5	3.5
87	83	459	324	124	117	110	86	789	97	15.6	13.2	5.4
18.2	16.6	55.8	39.1	29.1	7	5	25.1	15.6	9.7	2.7	1.5	0.53
17	13	17	17	16	9.5	1.7	14	16	17	17	17	17

caked)

EE	AEE	NDF	ADF	Lignin	WSC	Sugars	Starch	NCD	TA	Ca	P	Mg
114	**116**	–	–	–	–	**38**	**15**	**832**	**141**	**19.5**	–	**5.9**
107	113	–	–	–	–	37	12	829	139	18.9	–	5.8
121	122	–	–	–	–	40	17	836	143	20.4	–	6.0
5.3	3.9	–	–	–	–	1.3	2.3	2.7	1.6	0.58	–	0.08
5	5	–	–	–	–	5	5	5	5	5	–	5

extracted)

EE	AEE	NDF	ADF	Lignin	WSC	Sugars	Starch	NCD	TA	Ca	P	Mg
18	**27**	**125**	**91**	**14**	**107**	**100**	**24**	**904**	**69**	**3.9**	**7.4**	**3.0**
13	23	65	39	6	82	86	8	899	64	2.8	6.8	2.4
26	32	185	139	22	126	120	54	910	79	8.7	8.5	3.3
4.0	3.2	43.3	38.9	5.7	15.2	11.6	18.0	4.2	3.8	1.6	0.44	0.23
15	5	11	11	11	6	6	11	5	12	12	12	11

Nutritive values[1]

	ME	DOMD	Dig NDF	Dig CP	Eff N Dg		DM	GE	CP
	MJ	g					g	MJ	g

Soyabean meal extracted, dehulled (5-04-612 Soybean, seeds

Mean	–	–	–	–	–		**887**	**19.9**	**547**
Min	–	–	–	–	–		880	19.8	538
Max	–	–	–	–	–		892	19.9	552
SD	–	–	–	–	–		5.2	0.06	5.6
n	–	–	–	–	–		5	5	5

Soyabean, full fat (5-04-597 Soybean, seeds, heat processed)

Mean	**15.5**	**690**	–	**0.92**	**C**		**898**	**23.8**	**415**
Min	15.1	665	–	0.90			890	23.6	395
Max	16.0	729	–	0.94			924	24.1	429
SD	0.37	28.3	–	0.02			10.7	0.18	11.0
n	4	4	–	4			9	9	9

Sunflower seed meal (5-25-634 Sunflower, seeds with some hulls,

Mean	**9.6**	**603**	**0.45**	**0.87**	**0.80**		**898**	**19.5**	**336**
Min	8.6	549	0.37	0.85	0.73		887	19.0	302
Max	11.0	675	0.54	0.88	0.87		905	19.8	390
SD	0.96	46.8	0.08	0.01	0.056		7.7	0.29	31.4
n	6	6	4	6	5		6	6	6

[1]ME and DOMD per kg DM; digestibility values as coefficients; effective N degradability as a coefficient at a fractional outflow rate of 0.05 per hour - where coefficients have not been determined, the degradability group (A to D; see Glossary of Terms, page 3) is indicated.

[2]DM as ODM per kg FW; other values per kg DM.

Chemical composition[2]

EE	AEE	NDF	ADF	Lignin	WSC	Sugars	Starch	NCD	TA	Ca	P	Mg
g	g	g	g	g	g	g	g	g	g	g	g	g

without hulls, meal solvent extracted)

EE	AEE	NDF	ADF	Lignin	WSC	Sugars	Starch	NCD	TA	Ca	P	Mg
20	**31**	**109**	**67**	**8**	**–**	**105**	**34**	**922**	**70**	**3.0**	**7.9**	**3.1**
10	21	70	36	3	–	99	21	917	67	2.6	7.8	3.0
25	38	144	92	11	–	111	51	923	71	3.6	8.1	3.3
7.1	8.6	34.1	25.3	3.0	–	5.0	13.7	2.6	1.7	0.37	0.15	0.14
5	5	5	5	5	–	5	5	5	5	5	5	5
222	**229**	**122**	**82**	**8**	**84**	**76**	**15**	**924**	**54**	**2.7**	**5.9**	**2.4**
200	223	105	68	6	80	71	8	922	51	2.1	5.6	2.2
232	239	144	129	11	89	81	18	929	56	3.0	6.1	2.4
14.6	5.1	12.3	20.7	2.0	3.9	4.2	3.1	2.1	1.4	0.28	0.14	0.07
9	8	9	9	9	4	5	9	9	9	9	9	9

meal solvent extracted)

EE	AEE	NDF	ADF	Lignin	WSC	Sugars	Starch	NCD	TA	Ca	P	Mg
23	**27**	**473**	**328**	**75**	**66**	**–**	**3**	**633**	**71**	**4.8**	**10.8**	**5.8**
9	20	445	294	63	61	–	2	587	59	3.3	8.7	5.2
35	35	525	372	86	79	–	4	671	80	6.5	14.2	6.4
10.7	6.2	29.7	28.2	9.8	6.5	–	1.8	35.9	7.8	1.4	1.9	0.49
6	4	6	6	6	6	–	2	4	6	6	6	6

REFERENCES

ARMSBY, H. P. (1903) *The Principles of Animal Nutrition*, 1st Edition. Wiley, New York.

EDEN, A. and BUTTRESS, F.A. (1965) *N.A.A.S. Quarterly Review*, Spring Edition, 123-128.

EVANS, R.E. (1960) *Rations for Livestock*, 15th Edition. *MAFF Bulletin 48*.

HENRY, W.A. (1898) *Feeds and Feeding*, 1st Edition. W.A. Henry, Madison, Wisconsin.

KELLNER, O. (1905) *Die Ernahrung der Landwirtschaftlichen Nutztiere Verlagsbuchhandlung*. Paul Parey, Berlin.

KELLNER, O. (1909) *The Scientific Feeding of Farm Animals* (translation by Goodwin, 1909). Duckworth, London.

MAFF (1990) *UK Tables of Nutritive Value and Chemical Composition of Feedingstuffs*. Ministry of Agriculture, Fisheries and Food, Standing Committee on Tables of Feed Composition, Rowett Research Services, Aberdeen.

MORRISON, F. B. (1930) *Feeds and Feeding*, 15th Edition. F. B. Morrison, Ithaca, New York.

SCHNEIDER, B. H. (1947) *Feeds of the World*. Jarrett Printing Co., Charleston, West Virginia.

THAER, A. (1809) *Grundsatze der Rationellen Landwirtschaft*, Volume 1, Section 275. Die Realschulbuchhandlung, Berlin.

WOLFF, E. (1861) *Die Landwirtschaftliche Futterungslehre und ie Theorie der Menschlichen Ernahrung*. Cotta' scher Verlag, Stuttgart.

WOLFF, E. (1871) *Aschenanalysen von Landwirtschaftlichen Producten, Fabrik-Abfallen und Wildwachsenden Pflanzen*. Wiegandt und Hempel, Berlin.

WOLFF, E. (1894) *Landwirtschaftliche Futterungslehre*, **6**, Paul Parey, Berlin.

WOOD, T. B. (1917) *Composition and Nutritive Value of Feedingstuffs*, 1st Edition. Cambridge University Pitt Press, Cambridge.

WOOD, T. B. (1918) *Composition and Nutritive Value of Feedingstuffs*, 2nd Edition. Cambridge University Pitt Press, Cambridge.

WOOD, T. B. (1921) *Rations for Livestock*, 1st Edition. *MAFF Miscellaneous Publication 32*.

WOOD, T. B. and WOODMAN, H.E. (1932) *Rations for Livestock*, 7th Edition. *MAFF Bulletin 48*.

WOODMAN, H. E. (1948) *Rations for Livestock*, 11th Edition. *MAFF Bulletin 48*.

INDEX OF FEEDS

[1] of feed or parent material

INDEX OF FEEDS (cont.)

[1] of feed or parent material

INDEX OF FEEDS (cont.)

[1] of feed or parent material

INDEX OF FEEDS (cont.)

[1] of feed or parent material

INDEX OF FEEDS (cont.)

[1] of feed or parent material